Stage THIS!
Volume 3

Monologues,
Short Solo Plays
and 10-Minute Plays

Stage THIS! Volume 3
Monologues, Short Solo Plays and 10-Minute Plays

Finalists from the Playwriting Competition
"Stage THIS! 3: Monologue and 10-Minute Plays"
sponsored by
E-MergingWriters.com and Fn Productions

Edited by
Frank Blocker, Dana Todd and Sydney Stone

Dedication

The third volume of *Stage THIS!* is dedicated to the memory of Murray Scott Changar, who talked loudly and frequently at the television, who built strange worlds and even stranger plots with his imagination, and who loved all animals.

Murray Scott Changar entered his play *White Picket Fence* in the first *Stage THIS!* contest in 2005, but preferred to read, critique and discuss the plays instead of competing. We mutually decided to withdraw him from further competitions while he was in the semi-final round. He dove into the play selection process with us, critiquing and evaluating more than 100 plays. He followed that by helming two of the finalist plays in full production at the 78th Street Studio Theatre in Manhattan, directing the 2007 Audience Favorite Award Winner *Whatever Happened to…The Three Sisters.*

Though a dedicated New Yorker, he never forgot his family back home in St. Louis. His siblings and he shared a deep love and respect for their mother Shirley and father Henry—an inspiration to us all, having spent his *teen* years *twice* escaping World War II concentration camps. Murray Scott was a proud graduate of Webster College and remained good friends throughout his life with his favorite high school teachers, dramaturg and director Ron Cohen and his wife, Lynn, the celebrated character actress. He came to the Big Apple in 1977, performing at The McCarter in *Coriolanus*, American Theatre of Actors and Drama Committee Rep and landing a featured role in the movie *The Chosen*. His curly locks that filled the screen would abandon him soon after when he embraced directing, his proudest works being two off-Broadway productions: *Full Circle* and *Nelson and Simone: Out of Senses*. In 2003, he added another shingle to his door, penning a full-length play *The Gates of Helen* that premiered in Atlanta, a one-page play that was a winner in the Lamia Ink Festival, and his first 10-minute play, *Fence* (Short Attention Span Play Festival), all within a year. His last play, *The Noble Sons of Popeye*, was performed by Los Angeles' Circus Theatricals, and *Fence* was selected by 4th Meal Productions for presentation in the 12-Hour Play Festival.

But it was not resume line items where Murray Scott left his mark, but with the people around him. It is here where he will be missed the most: acting coach, editor, assistant, producer, therapist, shoulder, partner and friend. A person with so much passion for the success of his fellow man is a rarity.

He celebrated imperfection yet worshipped cinema's vision of perfection. He was strong enough to overcome many difficulties and a lifetime of health challenges, but could weep listening to a beautiful aria.

To continue his memory, we ask that you take time to think about what was important to him: that in the theatre, you must be allowed to fail to succeed—and the failures should be just as breathtaking as the success. Murray Scott also believed in the right to marry—marriage for all—as his proudest achievement was his long-term relationship, recognized legally by the City of New York as a registered domestic partnership.

Table of Contents

Foreword

Stage THIS! Volume 3: Monologues, Short Solo Plays and 10-Minute Plays is the third collection of playwrights offered by E-MergingWriters.com and New York-based theatre company Fn Productions. Employing theatre and playwriting professionals, we adjudicated 150 unique theatre pieces from around the world meant for either the 10-minute play genre or for the solo performer. All are appropriate for a classroom, audition or full technical performance, barring any prudish issues with language or content.

E-Merging Writers and Fn Productions' vision is to promote playwrights whose work should be seen and not just read. We are proud of the writers that we are promoting. We do not offer "best of" awards, but it should be noted that our judging panel were particularly impressed with these monologues: *The Right Not to Take Me Seriously* for its magnitude and power in such a short time frame, *Gone* for presenting a character typically relegated to victim as someone who inspires *us*, and *Psychic* for seducing us. Among the 10-minute plays, *All the Way* received the highest overall scoring from the preliminary round. It is rare to find a playwright who treats characters with such grace. The script *Just Because of the Umbrella* brought about some of the strongest responses during the final stages of our process. This Croatian playwright shows a mastery of the English language and uses subtext in an innovative way to guide the reader. All of the plays are rich in character and are certain to be savored by actors, directors and audiences.

How We Pick 'Em

For this year's competition, we decided to concentrate on monologues and short solo plays but also accepted 10-minute plays. Three different judges read each piece, ranked them in groups of 10-12 and also gave them a quality score rating on a scale of 1-10. Beyond the scoring system, judges were asked to identify plays for which they felt a passion. From there, several discussions took place before the following list of semi-finalists were named:

Action and Reaction by Jo-el Hennigh Doty
An American Novelist Lost In Paris by Adam R. Burnett
Bates by David Dudley
Bye by Chris Davis

Our lengthy review process includes multiple private reading sessions with professional actors who read the semi-finalists for our panel. These actors were invaluable in helping the plays come to life: Eric C. Bailey*, Gina Bonati*, Emilie Byron*, Charnele Crick, Cheryl King, Dell McLain*, Robbie Neigeborn, Cara Vander Weil, and Michael Yeshion.

Our judging panel came from a variety of resources: Gina Bonati*, playwright and actress; Charnele Crick, actress, singer, dancer; Lynn Phillips, writer and actress; Catherine Porter*, actress and co-founder of Peculiar Works Project, www.peculiarworks.org; Barry Rowell, playwright, co-founder of Peculiar Works Project and past Stage THIS! Finalist; Krista Severeid*, actress and producer; Cara Vander Weil, playwright, actress and past Stage THIS! Finalist.

Final selections are based on a months-long process of reading, re-reading, and listening to the plays. We're pleased to present the fruits of our labors to you, in this collection which includes irreverence, psychics, trained killers, the physically-challenged, prostitutes, dealers, spiritual leaders, lesbians, the existential...and a solo Christmas play that's really a good-sized one-act.

How to Read Play Format

In formatting the book for publication, we attempted to maintain the playwright's original style, wherever possible. As plays are mostly dialogue, varied spellings are acceptable in scripts to demonstrate accents or style of speech. For purposes of reading this book, and since realistic dialogue also requires creative punctuation, we have applied a few general rules. We use two different types of stage direction: the first applies directly to the character speaking; the second, indented further to the right, concerns others on stage. An ellipsis (...) may suggest a slight pause, a change in thought, or even a trailing off. A long dash, or *em dash* (—), at the end of a line may mean the character speaking is being interrupted or that dialogue continues after stage directions or another character's line.

For those not familiar with reading plays, we provide the following example:

Prose format:

Jessie Ruth whispered, "I love you!" She slowly took his hand. "Always, and—." A telephone interrupted her.

Jack rose to answer the phone.

Play format

JESSIE RUTH
> *whispering*

I love you.
> *she takes his hand*

Always, and—

> > SOUND: *telephone rings. JACK crosses to desk and answers phone.*

Important Notice Regarding Performance Permission and Rights

All inquiries should be addressed to the appropriate playwrights, whose contact information is included in the biography section of this book. Ownership of a copy of this book does NOT grant the purchaser any performance privileges. The plays in this collection are fully protected by copyright laws of the United States of America, and are subject to royalty as well as permission solely from the **playwright** or his/her designated agent. All rights, including professional, amateur, motion picture, recitation, lecturing, public reading, radio and television broadcasting, and the rights to translate into foreign languages, are strictly reserved. Purchasing this book does not grant purchaser the right to perform, adapt or otherwise use these plays without express written permission from the playwright. Use of *any* plays for any reason without permission or knowledge of the playwright is vulgar.

Important Notice Regarding Music

Any and all references to songs and song titles are merely suggested or provided as a reference by the playwrights. Rights to use such suggested song titles or song lyrics in the performance or production of a play or plays must be sought separately, and such rights are not implied to be or have been granted, now or in future, by authors or sponsors. Fn Productions and E-Merging Writers are to be held harmless, now and in future, by all parties, of any kind or nature, associated with the performance or production of a play or plays, from any claims or assertions arising or related to usage of songs, song titles or song lyrics. Check with the music publisher and with your theatre's administration.

E-Merging Writers and Fn Productions take great pride in promoting playwrights. We hope you enjoy these as much as we do.

Editors
Frank Blocker*‡, Director, E-Merging Writers
Dana Todd, Media Strategist, Co-founder of Newsforce, Inc.
Sydney Stone*, Producing Director, Fn Productions

---

* Member of Actors' Equity Association, Union of Professional Actors and Stage Managers
‡ Member of Dramatists Guild of America

Monologues for Men

Cosmic Judo
Alan L. Steinberg

Cosmic Judo was presented as part of the 2006 Short Attention Span PlayFEST sponsored by Atlantis Playmakers in Boston, Massachusetts.

Character
MIKE — 20-30

Time
The present

Setting
Mike's backyard

> *MIKE enters from upstage, wearing slacks and a tee shirt which reads "Cosmic" on the front and "Judo" on the back. He moves to the wooden chair on which there is a sign, "PEEPER BEWARE." The sign is turned so that the words are not visible to the audience. Mike carries a small matchbook-size box with razor blades in it that he then puts in his pocket.*

MIKE
> *standing by the chair, to the audience*
That ought to do it. If he comes back tonight—
> *motions behind him*
—he'll be one sorry sonofabitch.
> *lets out a deep breath, as if he's been doing very hard work*
That's what took so long. Doing it scientifically. Rationally.
> *moves downstage, mimes the actions*
Measuring the footsteps. Measuring the space between. Measuring how deep. Then figuring out how tall he was, how long his arms would be. And where he'd have to reach.
> *beat*
Big sonofabitch. Six-two, six-three. That really threw me. I had to do the calculations all over again. Always figured they'd be small. Little guys.

Insecure. That's why they did it. Got their kicks that way, because they're too scared to do it themselves. But this time we got lucky. Rained like hell last night and when we got out here we could see these footprints in the mud like it was a gorilla or something.

motions behind him again

I mean, here we are on this dead end street, with a backyard full of weeds and one scrawny tree and this straight board fence up over your head, and we're up on the second floor and it's maybe two o'clock in the morning, and all of a sudden my girlfriend gives out with this great big scream like she's just seen Dracula, and I turn around and here's this face hanging in the tree like it's a goddamn jack o'lantern, and for a minute or two it was like something out of a horror movie, let me tell you.

beat

I mean, it's the middle of the night, and here we are lying in bed with the window open and no clothes on, and doing, well, what you should be doing in private, and she looks up and sees this face grinning down at her.

MIKE begins to move towards the audience, taking out the box and opening it and taking out a razor blade and holding it up as he speaks.

And that's how come I'm out here like this, putting razor blades in a tree. And that's why it took so long. Doing it scientifically. Putting a blade exactly in the place where he'd have to reach.

MIKE puts the blade and the box away again, moves to the chair and turns the sign over to reveal the writing.

And that's why I've got this sign here: "Peeper Beware." She didn't want me to do it, my girlfriend. She was real unhappy with me. She said just put the blades in and let the bastard climb. Let the sonofabitch bleed to death, she said. That's how scared she was and angry. I can't blame her, in a way, since she was the one he was looking at, I guess. But I told her I didn't think that was right, even though I could see where she was coming from.

beat

You see, I've got this theory I call Cosmic Judo.

turns around to reveal the back of the tee shirt

Turn every force back on itself. Like a boomerang. That's why I went to all the trouble of making up the sign. That's why I'm going to nail it to the tree, right up where he can see it. Then if he climbs, it'll be *his* doing, *his* force, not mine. You see how that works? If he comes out again after hearing her scream like that; if he climbs up over the fence and gets to the tree and sees the sign and decides to do it anyway, then *he's* the one to blame, not me.

It's like that law about the conservation of energy—for every force there's an equal and opposite reaction—only this one is about morality. About doing what's right.

> *speaking faster, more intensely, as if what he's describing is happening*

The fence says this is private property, not yours, but somebody else's, somebody who doesn't want you here. But you decide to go past it. You decide to climb anyway. Break in, really. Then you look around. You think you're safe. You think you're winning. You think privacy and the law don't matter. So you go ahead and kind of tiptoe over ground that's not yours either, till you get to the tree, and then you see this sign and you know that somebody knows about you, knows you're here and doesn't want you to be. And still you decide to go ahead, to disregard the warning, to let *your* will, *your* desire take command.

> *pause, calmer tone*

You see now, that's why this sign is the key. Without it, it wouldn't be Cosmic Judo. Wouldn't be an eye for an eye, a tooth for a tooth. Without it, someone could think it was more like a tooth for a leg. Or a tooth for an arm, maybe. Some poor sonofabitch wanting to see someone naked maybe bleeding to death. What's the big deal? You go to any beach or swimming pool you see people prancing around just about naked anyway. You've got magazines full of half-dressed women. You've got porn sites everywhere. Maybe this guy thinks it's like looking at a painting or something. Maybe he thinks it's like he's worshipping women, worshipping their beauty. Maybe it's somebody who can't help himself even, like an addict.

> *beat*

That's why this—

> *he holds up the sign*

—makes all the difference. This means you can't be doing it mindlessly, like some kind of robot. This means you have to look at the sign. Read it. Think about it. Think about what it means. Think about the people who wrote it. Who took the time to warn you.

> *beat*

Like God did in the Garden of Eden. And then you go and you do it anyway. Go right past the sign and reach for the tree.

> *mimes reaching out*

Just like Adam. Only this time—this time—there's no apple there.

> *moves to the edge of the stage*

As you sow, so you shall reap.

> *points to the sign again*

Voila! Cosmic Judo.

> *pause*

My girlfriend thinks the sign will scare him away. I think she's kind of disappointed.

> *beat, speaking confidentially*

But me, I've got this feeling he's going to climb anyway.

> *begins to move back to the chair, stops, turns back*

That's why, tonight,

> *beat*

I'm going to leave the light on.

> *MIKE exits, carrying the sign.*

> *END*

The Right Not To Take Me Seriously
William Gebby

This monologue is taken from *The Confessional*, a full-length play concerning two Civil War veterans, Dr. Ian Ross and Rev. James Ferguson, who seek absolution in the intellectual nooks and crannies of Boston and Cambridge. *The Confessional* was produced by Inklings Theatre in Indianapolis, Indiana, February 2004. Jonathon Markanday played Ian Ross and Luke Renn played James Ferguson. Ian Ross, the 33 year-old son of Scottish immigrants, reminisces about his experiences as a surgeon in the Union army.

Character
IAN ROSS — disheveled and drinking from a whiskey bottle

Time
1867

Setting
A doctor's office in Boston

At rise, a circle of light on IAN ROSS.

IAN
I am a buffoon—a profligate—a doctor. Like my father and grandfather before me. I learned medicine from Harvard—a school under the impression Death is a gentleman. I carried this sentimental view into my practice. If Death had a face it belonged to Beacon Street's soft-spoken undertaker: Mr. Archibald Arbuthnot. Of course, Mr. Lincoln's war happened along.

IAN drinks, wipes his mouth with the back of his hand.

Bull Run taught me Death was no gentleman. It also—

He drinks again—forgets to wipe his mouth.

—taught me I was no doctor. Only a butcher-boy. In the slaughter-house of all slaughter-houses.

> *beat*

I was hacking away—stealing glances at the monument of arms and legs I was building—when two orderlies carried in a boy—his eyes shut—his shirt-front bloodied. They laid him on the table. I heard Death snigger at my elbow—felt him push his snout past my shoulder. I cursed, tore the shirt off the crimsoned white flesh, jabbed my finger at the wound and screamed: "Making me waste my time on someone as good as dead!"

> *beat*

The shocked orderlies apologized. They slid the boy halfway off the table. Stopped. His eyes were open—and a tear was pushing its way down his cheek.

> *beat*

He'd heard every word. Every—word.

> *beat*

He died before I could lie to him. I closed his eyes—but couldn't close my own. Nine inches of intestine were sticking out of his belly—looking for all the world like an umbilical cord.

> *beat*

If it had been eighteen years before—and he a newborn child—and I, his father— and both of us bloodied from birth, not death—I would have gone down on my knees beside him—placed my mouth close to his ear—whispered low—so low: "My little son, never, never go to war."

> *beat*

I am a drunkard. You have the right not to take me seriously.

> *Slowly—very slowly—IAN is engulfed by darkness.*

> *END*

Monologues for Women

Beer and Newspaper

Alex Broun

Beer and Newspaper was first produced in 2003 as part of "Blind City" at the Sydney Festival in Sydney, Australia, directed by Kym Weatherley and performed by Sophie Gregg.

Character
JAMIE

Time
Early morning

Setting
Street, downtown

JAMIE enters, feeling her way with a cane.

JAMIE
How we met.
I left my apartment at 8:35 am exactly as usual.
I came down the stairs of the complex and walked across Mulberry and into Baxter, past the fountain trickling on my left and the smell of garbage at the cafe where I sometimes buy my lunch.
As I reached the corner of Center, I felt a slight cool breeze, ruffling my hair – and a warm glow on my face, like someone had lit a match—then silence.
No cars, no traffic lights, no people.
Nothing, except the trickling of the fountain.
Then suddenly an explosion of sound.
A woman screaming—car horns, drowning each other out.
Footsteps, a man's footsteps, running towards me.
I'm knocked to the footpath by a middle-aged man in a thick jacket.
He grabbed my hand and tried to pull me up.
"Leave me alone.
I'm alright.

You're the one who's confused.
I know exactly where I'm going."
I checked my watch. 8:47 am.
I had three minutes to get to my bus stop.
He'd be waiting.
But first I had to get across Lafayette and the lights had stopped working.
I couldn't hear any cars moving so I stepped on to the road.
It was unsafe I know but all I was thinking is that I have two minutes to get to my bus stop or he'll be gone.
I took another tentative step.
Ten more quick steps and I reached the other side.
Now it was 8:49.
One minute!
I walked quickly down the sidewalk to Broadway and made it to my bus stop.
8:50 am exactly.
But where was he?
Where was the man who smells of beer?
Not badly—he's not an alcoholic—just a faint smell.
And only in the evening.
One or two after his hard day at the stock exchange.
And he always has a paper which he reads on the bus.
That's why I christened him Beer and Newspaper.
Because I didn't know his real name.
Now it was 8:52.
I had missed the bus.
But no.
Surely it had been delayed.
But then where was he?
Chanel and Leather Bag was there, standing on my right.
She catches the bus two before mine at 8:48am and she was still there. My bus must still be coming.
8:57.
Chanel and Leather Bag sat next to me : "Did you see the flash?
What did you think it was?"
I did not answer.
I sensed her embarrassment as she sees the cane I'm holding in my hand.
9:02 am.
Still no Beer and Newspaper.

Cigar and Umbrella arrived.

Almost fifteen minutes late.

"Somebody said they've blown up the Trade Center" I heard him say. "If they've blown up the Trade Center why didn't we hear the bang?" replied Chanel and Leather Bag.

9:15 am.

I couldn't bear it.

Where was he?

Someone else began to speak.

He shouldn't have been at my bus stop.

"I reckon it was a nuclear bomb."

What was he doing at my bus stop?

"One of those ones that just blows up the people and leaves all the buildings standing."

9:20 am!

I was going to scream.

Beer and Newspaper had caught a taxi to work or worse still he'd been hurt in the flash.

Then suddenly I heard it—about a block away.

A bus.

Where is Beer and Newspaper?

The bus stopped.

The doors open.

Was it my bus?

I'm just about to ask Cigar and Umbrella when I hear the driver: "Something's happened. Nothing's going downtown right now."

"Something's happened?"

But what?

And how will I get to work?

I'm already late.

Then at last—the rustle of Newspaper.

9:32.

Beer and Newspaper had arrived.

I could feel him looking at me.

Play it cool.

Blind and independent is mysterious, sexy.

Blind and needy is pathetic.

"I see you made it."

Was he talking to me?

"I was worried about you."

"Don't worry about me," I thought to myself, "it's everybody else who's running around like idiots."

But then Beer and Newspaper laughed and I suddenly realized that I said it out loud.

I was embarrassed but I could feel a smile growing on my face.

"Well that's alright then."

Beer and Newspaper was worried about me.

"Come on" he said, "no one's going anywhere today.

I'll walk you home."

I feel him gently take my arm.

I'm nervous, anxious, and very curious.

"Okay then" I heard myself say.

Together we walked over to the curb and stepped out on to the street.

JAMIE exits.

END

Cheryl
Lisa Stephenson

This monologue is from the play *Bedside Manners*. The play premiered as an Equity Showcase produced by Theater Rising, Ltd. in New York City at the Blue Heron Theatre, directed by Tom Franco and performed by Melanie Boland.

Character
CHERYL

Time
The present

Setting
A New England bed and breakfast, Room 3

CHERYL

I'm here to choose between two men vying for the same job. Regional senior vice president. The job offers benefits, one company car, two secretaries, multiple stock options. A retirement package that will make him look forward to old age. I already know who's going to be hired. The interview is pointless. It's the process that holds great interest.

Cindy and I arrived in New York at the same time. She graduated from a small college in Vermont where she met John, guest lecturer in the art department. I came to the city alone from the University of Chicago.

Our careers followed similar paths. Go-sees. Dropping off portfolios. Gallery openings over glasses of white wine. We sketched in the Park. Visited museums. Attended lectures at the New School.

Every year, on each other's birthday, we did a rendering of the birthday celebrant as a famous person. I sketched her as Queen Elizabeth, Olivia de Havilland and Marlon Brando. She painted me as Marilyn Monroe, Grace Kelly and Adolf Hitler.

We laughed until we cried. She was the sister I never had.

When Cindy and John decided to marry we shopped for her wedding dress together. I was her maid of honor.

Within a year they moved out of the city and bought a home in the burbs. She had a child.

I got a job at a large graphics company and finished my masters. When I got married Cindy was my matron of honor.

My husband and I saw John and Cindy whenever we could. Turkeys were carved. Trees were trimmed. Favorite books were shared and switched. For their anniversary I sketched them as Paul Newman and Joanne Woodward.

A year later, I called Cindy. John took the message. She never returned the call. I phoned almost every day and was very worried.

No need to have been. Everything was explained in a letter. Delivered on a Saturday morning with two bills.

"Dear Cheryl: I know I owe you an explanation. I've been unhappy with our friendship for many years. John and I find your behavior offensive and unforgivable. Especially last Christmas. You've caused many problems in our relationship. I never wanted you as a friend. I'm sorry we've continued as long as we have. I feel closer to my neighbors than I ever did with you. I was never comfortable with our friendship. I never felt that you were one of us."

Fifteen years is a long never.

And today? Their son, Steven Welles, is one of the two candidates for this job. His education is good. His qualifications are excellent. He's superb. I've had him flown to Boston for the pleasure of telling him that he didn't get the job. When he asks why, I'll simply mention that I knew his mother.

END

Geraldine
Michele Merens

Character
GERALDINE — an African-American woman in her fifties living in Milwaukee, Wisconsin.

Time
2006

Setting
Talking to her preacher after Sunday Service

GERALDINE
You know which one of my jobs I love most, though? Being someone's Shabbos goy. Every Friday just before sundown, I go into the homes of Jews, I turn out their lights, help with the meals, let them rest through their Sabbath.

Mostly, I'm Shabbos Goy for Dr. Cohen, an Orthodox Jew who lives on the East Side, on Prospect Avenue. Now it's hard to travel back and forth from one side of town to the other. But I said I would be willing if perhaps I could sleep on a cot or something on Friday nights and work through the Sabbath before I went home. And Dr. Cohen said "Okay," and every week since, it's become what I live for, my Shabbos time with the Jews. Every time I go, it's so quiet and peaceful in Dr. Cohen's house. And there, I got Martin in my head and Jesus, too, both of them talking to me non-stop when the Jews are out praying, or coming home and resting. And meanwhile I'm down scrubbing floors clean and doing my own praying with no one to interrupt what's in my head.

Now I'll tell you, real freedom in this world is when you're down on your knees. Some people come so far with money or whatever in this country, they think freedom's no longer having to clean their own floors. But they're wrong, they're exactly wrong, because you see, they've forgotten just what freedom can be when you're down there, cleaning. Just how much can be done when you're down so low that no one else is even noticing you, well, that's really free.

Besides, it's beautiful really, to be in that house every Shabbos, with its polished candlesticks and the bread in braids and the candles and Mrs. Cohen allowed to sit on her wicker chair on the four-season porch as if she were Queen of the house for a few hours a week. And Dr. Cohen in his library, reading his Jewish books, too. They're both dressed in their best clothes waiting in their house until sunset like children waiting for a party each week, and they're right. Every week it is like a party comes into that house, with more people dressed up in their best clothes coming to visit and soup cooking and bread baking and songs sung and dancing at every meal, you can count on it. Out of the dark and the quiet that hangs on the house for 24 hours, there's always this burst just at sunset, this orange bursting fireworks glow of noise and music and joy.

What a gift! What a job! To have all those hours each week to figure things out. When I'm down on the floor washing, or scrubbing pots at the sink, Martin sits in my head and I say to him, "Martin, isn't this nice what we got ourselves here?" And he says back to me, clear as can be, "Well, I told you all along it could be so. These Jews know the Promised Land." And I say back, "Martin you've surely been right all along. But isn't this nice, though?"

And I think being the Shabbos goy every week is no work, it's a pleasure, because it's so peaceful out there on Prospect Avenue. On Prospect, I can relax. There's no gunshot to hear and I'm not waking up every day hunched over, hearing the yells and crouching at the window, hoping no one I know is out on the street.

Where I came from, those streets on the West Side, there's so much fighting, and most times my daughter Sherilee and me, we didn't get to choose our fights neither.

Sometimes there's fights from the day your child's born. So you, the Mama, always have to be some kind of soldier where we live. A soldier and a Mama both, making sure your family is safe, right from the start. Even before they can walk, our babies got to learn to be still in Mama's arms and not cry out—even when the nasty boys come by in their cars dogging the streets and their boomboxes blaring filth onto your baby's ears, all that stuff about whores and wars and—and red blinking lights shining in your windows on your little ones just when you've finally gotten them off to sleep.

I was tired all the time when my babies were small. But it's not right, it's really not right. Don't put all the wars on us women and all the bodies on us and all the tears and all the work and all the gunfire where we live, and call us Mamas. Don't do that. That's a lie. Truth is, we're the soldiers. That's our lifework. The rest of the world gets it so wrong—calling us not soldiers but just black unwed Mamas, like we're standing at your doors asking for help. What's true is I'm at my door, facing a war every day and fighting for my babies. And fighting—that means squatting. That means squinting, sweating, looking behind you, looking in front of you at the same time, and sideways, sideways, what's coming up sideways. Using not just eyes to look, but ears, and mostly getting down, down, down, on the floor as close as you can to where you can hear the footsteps coming from all directions, any shaking, any noise, any car engine, any click of the gun in any direction, down low on the floor where they can only trip over you, not shoot. And meanwhile you're thinking all the time about how to get out of this war.

I'm not an ant either, down there on the floor, but a Queen Ant. The best ant. The Mama and the soldier ant. The general and the breeder ant. I'm both and I'm all of that. So give me the respect a Queen ant deserves—a soldier-general mother of them all, and don't call me nothing else. That's what I say.

I suppose you're going to ask me, "Where does that leave your boys, then? All your black boys, if women are doing the jobs of Mamas and soldiers both, all those Queen Ants, where we live?" "It don't leave them much," I'll answer. I tried to tell this to Ty, but Ty's a black man who can't see the world much differently than the world sees him. I said to Ty, "Get Martin in your head." But he couldn't understand. I even tried to send him over to the Cohens on Prospect one Sabbath. So that he could see what I saw there, live the peace that I knew there, but no, it didn't work out. He scared them on Prospect. "He's not like you, Geraldine," Dr. Cohen complained. Because his black shadow hit their wall differently than mine when the candles were burning, and they saw him different. "Too hungry-looking," they said. So too scary for them.

So I agreed when Ty said he wanted to join the Army and go fight overseas, even though my heart broke up some. Because if he goes to war somewhere else, away from these streets, well, then, maybe he can get time and space to figure it all out. Get his days of peace fighting someone else's war, not his own, all the time. Because there's no way for a black man to be a King on these streets in Milwaukee, in homes where only the Queen Ants are in charge. Just no way at all!

END

Gone
Paul Shoulberg

Character
TANYA

Time
The present

Setting
Wherever Tanya studies best

    TANYA
Alright. Alright. Alright.
    closes book
Got it. And go down the list and don't say nothin' unless I mess up. Even if I mess up, just let me work through it before—I'll let you know if I need your help. And I won't, 'cause I got this shit down. Alright. Alright. Alright. Glands. It's fuckin' on.
    beat
Adrenal—produces hormones—cortiscosteroid hormones, to be motherfuckin' exact—that do all kindsa important shit with the metabolism—chemicals in the blood—and various other things that aren't s'posed to be on the quiz. Pituitary—you want it? You ready for it? Helps out the adrenal glands, the thyroid, the ovaries AND the testes, increases absorption of water into the blood by the kidneys and it controls the shit outta some skin pigmentations. Blam. I got that shit? You know I do. I can go word for word with all of it. Best in the class and don't intend to slip.
    beat
Best part about becoming a nurse—other than bein' able to finally quit workin' at that bitch-ass Duane Reade—is havin' a job that can take you wherever the fuck you want. 'Cause I'm gonna tell ya—and you know me—you know how I am, I don't fuck around when I say what I gotta say— this place—this place here—no thanks. Seriously. People always sayin', "Where you gonna go, you leave the city?" Where am I gonna go?

For real? Somewhere where I don't gotta spend almost two hours catchin' the 6 every morning, transferring to the 4 or 5 and hopin' that bitch moves along at the right speed—'cause sometimes express just means We Ain't Stoppin, But We Ain't Movin'—and you finally get where you gotta be and it's like people everywhere runnin' into you, not sayin' "sorry" or "excuse me" or "how's your day?"—makin' you into someone that doesn't wanna say that shit, either.

    beat

I don't even smile no more.

    beat

So where am I goin' when I'm done with nursing school? Fuck if I know. But I'll have a good job and a car maybe—and if I don't, I'll be somewhere where I can walk at my own pace—where I got room to breathe—where I can look at someone and say, "Ain't this weather a bitch?" and they'll say—like—"Could be worse"—and that'll be that and that's all it needed to be. And then—and then I could calm the fuck down. Relax. Live like a human, adrenal glands and all. Did I mention the thyroid? Its functions? No. I didn't. 'Cause it's too fuckin' easy and I ain't gonna waste anyone's time with it. But trust me when I say I got the thyroid, bitch. Got it down.

    beat

For real—for real—for real I can't even understand why everyone and their broke-ass cousin is movin' here. I've been here forever. Forever. And I can tell you true—it ain't shit. I mean—maybe somewhere in Midtown—if you got cash fallin' out your ass or somethin'—maybe that's a good life. But even then, you could live it three times larger somewhere else. Like—I don't know—Wisconsin or somethin'. Yeah. Maybe I'll go there. But everyone else—like—all these motherfuckers runnin' around—it's like—what? What is it? Why you tryin' to act like this is somewhere you're lucky to be. Comin' out from Texas, Colorado, California—thinkin' New York is gonna be their best and final chapter. The place they take a stand and become the person they've always wanted to be.

    laughs

Actor? Shit. How many actors you know doin' any actin'? My girl—my girl, Monica—she thinks she's an actor. Last time I checked, she was actin' like she worked the register at Whole Foods. Ain't tryin' to hate or nothin'—I mean—you know—do your thing or whatever, but don't be comin' here pretendin' you chasin' the dream—then spend every second doin' somethin' else just to survive. I say I'm gonna be a nurse, I'm gettin' mine. Be one soon. You say you wanna act—act, motherfucker. You say it's too hard to act here—go somewhere where it ain't. But don't be comin' here, fillin' up the sidewalks, the trains, the neighborhoods with your lies. See—see—for every one of your half-ass dreams—I gotta move further north. Raised in Harlem—until the actors, the painters, the dancin'-ass bitches crept in. Now I'm in the Bronx—6 to the 4 or 5—slow-ass ride— never get a seat—you know the drill. Jus' sayin'.

> *beat*

Don't matter, though. I'm out soon. Shit—maybe I'll just swap places with one of them Colorado-Texas bitches. Got a nice little pad—four hundred fifty feet—roaches, rats, kids screamin' in the halls—only twelve hundred a month. You got, what—two bedrooms, one for your cat—patio—washer and dryer on site—maybe even in the apartment—parking place—for what? Half as much, I bet. If that. Yeah—bring your ass here—good fuckin' luck.

> *beat*

The pancreas is under the stomach and connected to the small intestine. Most important gland in the digestive process. You know I know, so don't even try to fuck with my shit.

> *beat*

I'll miss the food, though. Ain't gonna lie. Don't get me wrong—ready to get out soon as I can, but—not too excited about—you know—Applebee's, Olive Garden—whatever the fuck they try to pass off as food in the Midwest. I mean—never been there—but I know. See how excited everyone gets when they first come out here. We got the real deal—none of this franchise shit. Go to one of them Dominican neighborhoods— around Washington Heights—get you a whole chicken and some plantains. Yeah—yeah—you know what I'm talkin' about. And we got this Chinese place around the corner—you can't fuck with it—it's that good. Serious—like—they got these egg rolls—don't tell me you know unless you been there. 'Cause—'cause—I know.

> *beat*

I know.

> *beat*

The pineal gland—extends from the third ventricle of the brain, cone-shaped, takes care of your melatonin needs, y'all. Yeah—yeah—I got this shit.

> *opens book, starts reading*

Got this shit down.

END

I Witness
Joan Anderson and Dorothy Sanders

Character
WOMAN — in her 40s or 50s

Time
The present

Setting
Any place

> *A WOMAN, dressed professionally and carrying a large purse, walks to the middle of the stage. She stops and begins to search for something in the purse, looks up at the audience and then speaks as if in explanation:*

WOMAN

Well, you have to understand…I saw him. I actually saw him do it. No, no, no, not the rape. I didn't see that. I saw him strangling her in broad daylight. It was so unreal, it took me a few seconds to even comprehend it. But when he turned and looked up at me just for that second…I'll never forget his eyes. Even after all these years. Never.

I backed my car out of that alley so fast I that I hit fences and garbage cans the whole way. I called the police from my car phone. Maybe she was still alive. Maybe they could save her.

It was my neighbor, Carolyn. Such a lovely person. She'd been out jogging. A lot of people in our neighborhood did that every day.

She left behind two small children. I don't even have words to describe how awful it all was. I gave them a description of the man. The police. It was amazing. The artist made this perfect drawing of him. It even scared me to look at it. That's how real it was.

Everyone in the neighborhood was stunned. No one would go out alone. We were afraid to even get our mail.

You can imagine how relieved we were when the police found a suspect. That's when they called me in to see if I could identify him. I did go. I did it. There he was, number four, standing there looking just like the drawing. Just the way I remembered him that day in the alley. They told me he was the man from the lawn service. I didn't know him but he was a regular down the street.

I testified at the trial. I was very nervous but I wanted to do it for Carolyn and her family. I was stunned when the jury sentenced him to death. I wasn't against the death penalty. It's just knowing that the jury made that decision based on my testimony. You have to understand, I was the only eyewitness. But I just kept thinking about Carolyn and that helped me through it. Her husband and the children moved away after the trial to be closer to family, and I didn't think about it so much anymore. For years. And then, it was time.

It was in the paper. I read that one of Carolyn's kids, the oldest one, was going to the execution. I kept taking Valium that day. I don't know how many pills, but it didn't help. I couldn't stop thinking about it. It haunted me for months. My doctor put me on Prozac, but that didn't really help either.

It's just that he kept saying he was innocent. But I saw him. I knew what he did. Even though there was no other evidence, I knew the truth. I couldn't understand why his family kept trying to get a DNA test even after he was dead. It was over.

I did go to his grave. I did. I never thought I would do that. Visit his grave. But, I had to tell him how sorry I am...how very, very sorry. He really did look just like the drawing. Just exactly the way I remembered him.

They opened the case again. Oh my God, the cameras, the phone calls...they wouldn't stop. And asking me how I felt. I wouldn't talk to them. None of them.

I'm sorry Carolyn that they didn't find your murderer. I'm sorry that they executed an innocent man. I'm sorry I ever drove down that alley that day. I'm sorry that I saw the murderer and I'm sorry that...that...

> SHE suddenly grabs her purse and starts anxiously searching it. Her hand stops. She slowly pulls out a gun and looks at it and then looks calmly back at the audience.

There's not enough Prozac in the world to help me forget that HE saw me.

> SHE puts the gun in her pocket and exits.

> *END*

JD
Lisa Stephenson

This monologue is from the play *Bedside Manners*. The play premiered as an Equity Showcase produced by Theater Rising, Ltd. in New York City at the Blue Heron Theatre, directed by Tom Franco and performed by Kathleen Dunn.

Character
JD

Time
The present

Setting
A New England bed and breakfast, Room 3

JD
I remember the day John Cheever died. And the day James Brady took a bullet for Ronald Reagan. And the day PanAm crashed near Lockerbie. I remember them because my own life was tinged with death on each of those days. As frequent as it is, it never becomes natural.

People hire me to do what they can't. People pay me to be discreet, dependable, reliable and effective. My fee reflects all of those things. After I complete my work the reports in the daily newspaper are the same. "Unusual activity was not reported." "There are no suspects." My stamp of excellence is remaining unknown.

This is how it works. Sometimes I move into an area. Get familiar with the neighbors. People trust me. I watered plants for a couple; my first hit that looked like a double suicide. My hair changes color, length and style. I've looked fifteen years older and ten years younger. I've been pregnant five times. In a wheelchair once. I've been to fabulous metropolitan cities and to country towns that didn't even have a post office. I've flown to and from London in the same day.

I've kidnapped children for parents who weren't granted joint custody. My fee for dealing with small living creatures is twice what it is for just making sure people are dead. I come and go quietly. I'm never too friendly. I never say much.

In the beginning my conscience had to readjust. But today's morality comes in a do-it-yourself kit. You do what you need to do if it makes you happy. If it makes you money. If it gets you through. Honesty is a policy that won't get you far.

I had a client last year who lent a business associate $50,000. It was a verbal agreement. A gentleman's agreement. Nobody is a gentleman. My client eventually wanted the dough back to save his business.

The borrower was evasive. Unreturned calls. Ignored letters. My client was informed that he would get the money. Eventually. It was even guaranteed in the debtor's will.

My client is a reasonable man, but impatient, and an unfortunate car accident happened early one Saturday morning. The guy who owed him the money was driving to the country. So many crashes happen in inclement weather. My client's business has completely recovered.

Tonight will be easy. A man has discovered that his wife is cheating. I'm going to hear the Boston Symphony. I'll sit with her and her new lover. Box seats have never been my favorite. We'll have an informal, friendly chat. They'll think I'm a new friend. After giving my client more information than he needs I'll wait for further instruction.

Rule number one. Crime does pay. Rule number two. Don't talk to strangers. There is no rule number three.

END

A Peace of Candy
Marie Mastrangelo

═══

Character
CANDY WARREN — 36, small waist, nice rack, long legs, wearing a too
        tight, too short spandex dress

Time
The present

Setting
A wrecked adobe church in a thumbnail town on the indeterminate fringe
of time

═══

        CANDY walks up the aisle and stands before the blue-eyed,
        weeping Jesus. She reads the inscription above the altar:
        "Charity, Chastity, Devotion and Faith." She self-consciously
        tugs down at the hem of her dress.

    CANDY
Let me start out by saying I never asked you for nothing. Not when they
put me in that shit hole foster home, not when that prick Louie broke my
arm, not even when I got that lump...and between you and me, that was
the number one, all time, fucked up thing to do. How the hell was I
supposed to work without one of my essential tools of arousal?
      indicates her breasts
These girls aren't just accessories, you know. Who ever heard of tricks
without tits?
      looks down
Hey, it wasn't easy working in the service industry. The hours suck, you
get no holidays. Still with all the obstacles, I think I did pretty good. I
always sent those guys home happy. Did you or did you not see smiles?
All right, then. It's because I said to myself: Candy, give it all you got, you
only got one life. An extra two, an extra three minutes, lick hard, look
them in the eye, kiss their ass, whatever, I always said yes. I gave, dammit!
I gave a lot. A hell of a lot.

clears her throat, tries a different approach

You remember that guy outside of Lesko's? Always hanging around on the corner, my corner. Freakin' ten below and he doesn't have a coat—nothing, no sweatshirt, not even a towel—what was his name? We called him ass wipe, but I think his real name was Cooper. One day, I said to him, "Give me twenty minutes, you'll be warm, I promise." Next thing you know, he has the best fucking coat on the Lower East Side. That's because I put my heart, my hands and my tongue into it. Two hundred dollars in two minutes and no offense, but that john saw you, Mary and at least two major archangels.

laughs to herself

Ah, what the hell, you're going to do what you want, anyway. I mean, I didn't exactly get to be a ballerina. But I did the best I could.

beat

Every woman has to be a whore at least once in her life. Come on, don't be mean, you know you want me around. I could make you very happy.

looks around, there's nothing but dead air

Don't shut me out!

> SOUND: Suddenly, a car horn honks repeatedly outside the little church.

I knew it! I knew you wouldn't mess me up.

> CANDY rushes back down the aisle to meet her ride. She looks over her shoulder.

Thanks, Baby, thanks.

END

Psychic
By Beth Kander

Psychic was first read as part of the Fondren Theatre Workshop New Play Project in July 2005, produced by Fondren Theatre Workshop in Jackson, Mississippi, directed by Diana Howell and performed by Bettye Edwards.

Cast
PSYCHIC

Time
The present

Setting
A corner of a sidewalk in a cold Northern city, present day

> *Lights up on PSYCHIC, who sits in a rickety chair on the sidewalk. Beside her is a tattered but elegantly-lettered sign which reads "Madame Madeleine, Psychic. Palm Reading."*
>
> *PSYCHIC begins to cough—a loud, hacking cough. She gradually ceases coughing, moving her eyes over the audience slowly, expression somber. She makes a full sweep of the room before speaking.*

PSYCHIC

I won't call out to draw you in. Some of the other mediums do—they will call out their methods…their means of otherworldly communications, tea leaves or tarot or bones. They want customers, anyone with money. I only want to read the fortunes of those who take the time to seek me out. I do not like props. I read palms for thirty years in Jackson Square in New Orleans, until the water-witch came, and the winds blew me here, to this cold place. Cold and silent, not haunted like my New Orleans. No, you don't need any props to be in touch with the supernatural in the land of Creole and voodoo. It's in the air. It's in the streets. It's everywhere in the Quarter and its shadows.

SHE holds her hand aloft, uncurling her fingers, studying her own palm.

Palm reading. Palm reading is not just about hands. It is about faces, breathing patterns, reading the whole person. No props, no gimmicks. Just the person and their destiny, right there. There is a certain power in the hand, though. My hands. Your hands. An identity fit between your fingers, curving into your palm. A hand can tell you a lot about the future, often because it can tell you a lot about the past and the present.

SHE clenches her fist and rotates it.

I remember my father's hands – dirty fingernails from hard labor, clenched fists, rough knuckles from bar fights. His hand could tell you a lot about who he was, what he did, where he had been – even if you weren't a psychic. My father didn't believe in psychics. Called them psychos, or worse. Witches. Heretics. There was no God in his life, but there was plenty of fear of Satan and hellfire and brimstone, and he clutched it all in his hands.

SHE is suddenly overtaken by coughing and cannot speak for a moment.

I remember on the day my sister died, my father's fingernails cutting into his palm, mourning and punishing and telling his whole life. How he loved her. How he hated himself for hitting her.

SHE unclenches her fist, holds hand aloft in a "stop" position, then slowly drops it.

But that is not future. That is past. And while a hand can tell you much of the past, I am not interested in the past. I am much more interested in the future. Even when people do not stop and ask me to tell them their fate, I catch glimpses of their future. I can hear it in their conversations, smell it in their skin, feel it almost like I could feel New Orleans. All the joy, all the pain, the singing tingling of their destinies catches the light and reflects itself on me. But perhaps...perhaps it is reflection and reflection only. I am old now, and I no longer know some things. I no longer know if my intelligence or my insanity is what informs me. I no longer know if I am holding up a mirror to those who seek my insight, or holding the mirror up to my own haunted face. I no longer know when I see a young woman in pain, bruised, fearful, if the pain I am feeling is hers...or my sister's...or my own. An angry man, storming by me, sending angry energy lashing out in waves that break across me—he is a stranger, and he is my father.

SHE trembles a little, perhaps lost in a moment of memory, or clarity; perhaps a moment of dementia.

Sometimes I am relieved that few people stop and seek my counsel these days. I have never been able to see my own future, but I hope for a quiet one. No disturbances. I want just to be left alone. Unless...

Voice wavering, PSYCHIC's last line is delivered to no one, or to anyone:

...you want me to tell you your fortune?

LIGHTS fade.

END

Short Solo Plays

All the Pretty Little Horses
Robert Paul Laudenslager

All the Pretty Little Horses is an adaptation of a lullaby. Early, darker versions originate from an African-American slave as sung to her master's children; the lyrical content luridly described distinctions between the master's children for whom the singer was forced to care, and the singer's own neglected baby who yearned for its mother. The well-known, modified children's lyrics, however, lack this heartbreaking venom. These lyrical discrepancies parallel the disillusionment one suffers in the face of age and death, as compared to childhood's innocent joys.

Cast
OWAIN — a man in his sixties

Time
The present

Setting
A small, dirty, empty room

> *OWAIN stands. Over the course of the play, OWAIN shrinks into a small ball, fetal position, on the stage.*
>
> *Into the air, OWAIN outlines pictures with his fingertips. He sees these outlines blossom into vibrant images. OWAIN draws a flower.*

OWAIN
Tick. Tick. Tick. Tick. Tick. Tick. Tick.
    A flower. A lilac. White petals...four and then hundreds. Unpruned, from the wasted wood of the old room, the flower blooms and moves and grows and swells and bends and wilts and slowly dies, showering flower petals floating falling, finally sinking far and heavy deep into the corner of my eyes, melting, flowing down my cheek and toward my lip and I want to taste if they are sweet. I haven't seen those in years.

> *OWAIN sticks his tongue out, tries to taste the flower. OWAIN draws a horse.*

Tick. Tick. Tick. Tick. Tick. Tick.

A horse. Large. Brown hair. It's very coarse. It rears and neighs, stumbles and bows, emaciated by the heat and wanting some water, fervently searching the sand and sits, bending at the waist shrinking smaller and smaller, sapless, a pony, a male, a colt, its tiny tail fighting the bees and butterflies, crying for its mother and it's perfect. And when I age I cover the colt with gold or glowing silver and mount the monument on my wall while all the children come to play because I hug them and give them bottled waters and I'm their favorite. And they bring their parents with the *back thens* and the *I remembers* and I watch the children whistling their favorite lullabies, wishing I had lilacs for them to pick and wishing the bottles weren't empty.

> *OWAIN rubs his fingers on his gums. OWAIN draws a boy.*

Tick. Tick. Tick. Tick. Tick.

A boy. Small. Little Owen. I watch him, wave, he climbs the golden colt and smiles, the boy looked silly on the horse, the ride, holding on to save his life and never letting go the flowers picked from behind the park benches and then off he spins and I wait one, two, three, four, five, six, seven, eight, nine, ten, eleven, twelve, thirteen, fourteen, fifteen, sixteen, seventeen, eighteen, nineteen, twenty, twenty-one, twenty-two, twenty-three, twenty-four, twenty-five, twenty-six, twenty-seven, twenty-eight, twenty-nine, thirty, thirty, thir— I smile and wave at Owen and he still looks silly but I smile anyway, and the widow, the lady I assume to be a widow, smiles at me and looks and says *is he yours* and I give her a *nephew, yes, his name is Owen* and *its still his first time, he's young* and the widow with her *my baby boy is three rows back in the cart with the lamb*, and twenty-eight, twenty-nine, thirty, thir— I smile and wave at Owen, there again, more comfortable, and the widow with her *I remember doing this growing up* and *My first time* and I smile but I look through her, in the heat it's dry and hot and I've never been this thirsty and I want a vendor with the boxes but the lines from the carousel enclose the courtyard and the widow with her *they're already less nervous, they grow up so fast* and I look at my watch and tick, thir— I smile and wave at Owen and I rear up, big smile, count one, two, three rows back, the widow's baby boy, smile, wave at him, too, thinking I looked so hard I almost missed Owen spinning and laughing, laughing like children laugh, that belly bursting tickle laugh on their back covering their faces from the flowers and feathers tickling their noses, and more attentive I look at my watch and twenty-seven, twenty-eight, twenty-nine, thirty, thir— I smile and wave at Owen laughing, riding, spinning and wanting to ride behind him pointing, laughing at the widow with our *ugly old lady*s and we ride up down up down up down up down up down up down, searching for the drink vendor, laughing, and the widow with her *if only*s, and my teeth hurt from the tartness of the candy but still I eat, still no vendor, and the heat flowing falling, finally sinking into the park, into my sides, into my stomach until it stirs up through my throat and I bend so my tummy doesn't hurt and I look at my— I smile and wave at Owen slowly slowing circling spinning less, and *how apt the ride stops*, the curving coming to a halt and all the horses stopping and glowing from the children's sweat, Owen's sweat, my teeth hurt and my stomach stings so I bend to make it better and my *yes, I'm really that thirsty*, I'm really that thirsty, staring at the sweat, smacking the flies away from my glistening head, pulling Owen from the ride and wishing my watch had broken.

OWAN draws a house.

Tick. Tick. Tick.

My home. Smallest. No garden. No horses. Playing with the children laughing, tickling, and finding the full bottles, guzzling, eating the gooey sweets from the park, I like candy, but our teeth ache and we eat more anyway and keep tickling, telling tales of what my mother did when my father died and me with my *I remembers* and reminiscing of My First Time, rolling in the yard with the sweat and mud, the heat's hot, and I smile and wave at Owen, him and his *what's this* and giggling *that's a caterpillar*, and Owen says *they're ugly* but I remark *they grow into beautiful butterflies*, and the sweat drips between his eyes toppling from the tip of his nose and Owen with his *butterflies grow into ugly caterpillars* and silly boy, I smile and laugh because I know it doesn't work that way.

OWAIN draws a bottle.

Tick. Tick.

A bottle. Empty. It's empty, so we go home, take Owen home with the *Owen, it's time* and the solemn silence of the car, starkly contrast from the day, driving through the countryside, and the big brother in the house bellowing his *what the fucks* and throwing sweaty hands into my eyes with his *fucking fucks* and I cover my face and ears because those are bad words hitting hurting falling on the ground crying calling yelling not my face and his hands on my belly with his *did you touch him* and me *no I didn't touch him* and rolling screaming yelling spinning my eyes spinning and the sweat from his red knuckles ripping and his heavy fists heaving into my head reddening making sounds like bees buzzing that buzz before they die, the gross sounds of crunchy carrions, that crunch crunch crunch and dreaming of the child changing into a lamb becoming a butterfly that turns into an ugly caterpillar and crying because I know it doesn't work that way.

> *Pause. OWAIN rubs his fingers on his gums. OWAIN smacks away flies. He cries like a baby.*

The ground. Cold. Hard. Smelling the bitter rotted wood and watching the dying widows weeping from the window, so thirsty and sinking hard and heavy into the corners of the room with my hand in my hair so coarse and corpse-like and I remember my mom did this to comfort me when I was a baby, stomach splitting, fingers dry from bottles empty and my watch won't stop screaming.

Tick.

END

Barsha Badal
Asher Wyndham

Barsha Badal was staged at the 16th Annual City Festival at Cabaret Theatre in the Temple of Music and Arts in Tucson, Arizona, March 2008, directed by Meg Tully and starring Amrita Ramanan. The play was also performed at Theatre 54 at Shetler Studios in New York City, February 2008, for spork* A Festival of Short [mixed] Plays, presented by Mixed Company & FORwardMOVEment, directed by Asher Wyndham and Shetal Shah and starring Shetal Shah*.

Cast
BARSHA BADAL — an Indian (not Native American). Mid 20s to early 30s. She wears a salwar kameez. She has the bindi. She has a narrow scarf (dupatta) over her shoulders and flip-flops or sneakers on her feet. Her hair is tied back. A bangle or two.

Time
Summer, present day

Setting
Outside the office of Cheap Sleep Motel, somewhere (nowhere) in Nebraska, a lawn chair, a small radio on the floor beside the chair, boy's toys scattered everywhere: Thomas the Tank Engine trains and accessories, toy plane, tractor, truck, etc.

Note
If a director would like to consider adding the unseen characters to the play, s/he is encouraged to contact the playwright.

> *BARSHA BADAL enters chasing her (unseen) little son who is running away from her. SHE is carrying a plastic laundry basket at her side. It is full of dirty clothing belonging to her son and husband.*

BARSHA BADAL

Miland! Miland!

> *SOUND of a tractor. SHE stops the driver, "Mr. Jackson,"
> waving with her free hand.*

Mr. Jackson! Stop! Miland, do you want to go for a ride? Drop Thomas the
Tank Engine. Mr. Jackson's in his big tractor! He'll drive you through the
field and park so you can pet all those fat cows! Would you like that? You
want me to come along? I would, I would, but I have to get to these
stinkies. Go along, Miland. Miland! WATCH OUT FOR THE BICYCLISTS!
Sorry!

> *addresses offstage as if speaking to her husband, Niraj.*

Niraj, husband, look. A lot of bicyclists. Here come some more.

> *waves at the "bicyclists."*

They're going someplace. Across America, probably.

> *pause*

Lucky them.

> *addresses "Mr. Jackson."*

What's that Mr. Jackson? Oh sure. Miland likes rocket pops. Sure, take him
to the store. He doesn't need to be back soon. It'll be boring here for him. I
am just doing laundry.

> *with a playful frown, raises some laundry*

And later I have some rooms to clean.

> *waves*

Goodbye Miland!

> *SOUND of the tractor starting up and driving away. SHE
> tidies up—picks up toys. And then sits and looks for coins in
> pockets of pants. After a moment she turns on the small radio
> beside her. She turns the stations. Snippets of a commercial, a
> rock song, etc. She finds Diana Ross's "I Am Coming Out." She
> neglects her laundry and sings along for a while. She sets the
> coins aside, and stands to dance to the music—until she turns it
> off in reaction to her husband Niraj stopping her. She mouths
> "Sorry" and returns to cleaning out pockets.*

Niraj, husband, how's the Jacuzzi tub? Not hot enough? Stop complaining!
With all those Jacuzzi suds, it looks like you're in a bubble bath. Relax. We
have had our U.S. citizenship for a week now. Celebrate! It's slow time at
Motel Delhi. I know, it's not called that. It's called Cheap Sleep Motel.

Open another Bud. No. I don't want one! I have laundry, look, to do. I can get a lot done this morning.

glum

Now that the County Fair is over.

SHE stares out into the audience as if staring across a road.

The Ferris wheel is not up across the road, spinning around. No more bright lights. No more baby animals. Ponies. Piglets. Chicklets. I miss the baby goats with the little horns. They were so cute! I miss the cotton candy and the funnel cakes and the French fries and the lemonade and the funnel cakes and the cotton candy and the lemonade and the French fries. I just repeated myself!

a light laugh

I miss the teacup ride. Miland vomited caramel corn all over me, but the spinning was so so so much fun! I miss the bumper cars! I bumped you real good, didn't I? Is your neck still hurting you? Sorry, my dear. Turn your neck like this—Good.

lowers her head

The County Fair is over. The excitement is over. Back to normal.

pause

Our guests had a great time. Especially the teenagers. Partying in the parking lot, smoking in their pick-ups. They kept us up into the early hours. We made a lot of money. Greenbacks. Smackaroos. After expenses and repair to a wall, we would have a lot of money saved, right? No? Oh, I didn't expect that. That's okay. We have to wait. Until next County Fair? Another year—another year—waiting?! Oh, Brahma.

annoyed and saddened

I do, I do want that RV—that you promised—promised—me at the Immigration Office. It would be nice to just pack up my things and just go away, go out onto the road and explore, explore America. Yes, with you, my husband. Your brother Mani can watch the motel while we're away. I would love to sightsee—like Sacagawea.

Perhaps she finds a Sacagawea coin.

I want to see—everything. Yeah. The Redwoods of Cali. The Great Salt Lake. Yellowstone Park. Oh, not to forget Wall Drug and the Corn Palace in South Dakota! Maybe?

pause

Well, if we can't take a cross-country trip, maybe we can explore Nebraska a little bit more. Maybe we could go to Lincoln, again, and look at the

Bateman paintings in the shops. Go hand-in-hand, you and me. Like Aishwarya and Salman. Niraj, husband, what do you think about that? About what? Seeing Nebraska. Maybe?

> *pause*

Maybe.

> *pause*

Hey, maybe we could stop by Walgreens and get some good shampoo. Herbal Essences. Aroma Therapy.

> *like an ecstatic woman from a commercial for Herbal Essences.*

Yes! Yes! Yes!

> *she snaps out of her thought of being in a commercial.*

Too far from here? I'll drive. No?! I only crashed the car once. Just once into the farmer's fence.

> *an obvious lie*

I just want...shampoo. Please don't get mad, Niraj. I do love you. I am thankful. I am blessed with Nebraska. Who wouldn't be? Enjoy the Jacuzzi. Splish-splash.

> SHE looks inside more pockets, finds coins—and then finds her
> husband's wallet. She makes sure that Niraj does not see her so
> she can steal a few bills. She drops the wallet in the basket in
> reaction to her husband turning to look at her.

Hunh? What? The flowers? Yes, yes, I received the flowers from old Mrs. Paulson. She was crying when she brought them. Mrs. Paulson will miss Mother. Best of friends, they were. Taking long walks down the road. Even when it was raining.

> *pause*

I miss the rain. I said, I miss the rain. One time, one time when it was your turn to run the front desk and fold the towels, it was raining and I went out. I didn't sneak out! I told you—I did—but you were too busy watching that Batista Smackdown on WWE wrestling. No worries! At first it was a drizzle. And then it came down. Hard. Loud. On the pavement. On the carport. So, I went home and put on my rubber boots and got my Mickey Mouse umbrella with the ears. The one that Babar brother sent me as a souvenir. I went for a walk, like on a Sunday stroll, but it wasn't Sunday. It was Tuesday, a boring Tuesday. I stopped at the tractor and farm supply store to get out of the rain. Inside, there was this woman, a big woman in overalls, who said *a butch "Hello"*

"Hello." She asked me my name. Can you believe that? A complete stranger. "Barsha Badal," I said. "Barsha. Sounds like Marsha, like Marsha from The Brady Bunch. 'Oh, my nose! Oh, my nose!'"

a light laugh

She asked, "What's an Asian tourist doin' in Nebraska?" Asian tourist!

chuckles to herself

"Oh, no. I am from down the road. I work at Cheap Sleep Motel."

"No offense."

"What can I get ya, Barsha?"

"Just, uh, browsing,"

"We got a discount on selected wrench sets, aisle six."

chuckles again

So, there I was in this store for the first time, the only customer, walking up and down the aisles. Shelves full of strange farm stuff. My hair and umbrella were dripping wet. The rain was pounding on the steel roof. The rain must have done something to the lights. They were out. And it was pitch black. I was like, "Get me out of here. This is very spooky."

pause

And then they were up again.

pause

Niraj, did you know that chewing gum is sold at a tractor and farm supply store? I asked the woman does the store always sell Bubblicious, and she said, "Yes." I think I'll go to that store again to get Bubblicious.

SHE checks more pockets for coins.

I miss Mother. She never got to live that long in America. She never really experienced the American Dream. What? Yes, not like us. Niraj and Miland.

pause

And Barsha. We got something special going on here in Nebraska. Cheap Sleep Motel. Better than Super 8. A nice motel here.

an obvious lie

What's the point of re-incarnation—rebirth as a peacock under a banyan tree—when you can live one life in America? Everyone's happy in America.

SHE scans the audience as if scanning the motel and its property. She stands.

After work, I think I'll go for a walk. Up to the gas station to get a Snapple and a bag of Fritos. Okay? I, uh, I just want to go out on a stroll and see my surroundings.

> *SHE scans the audience.*

Corn and cattle fields. Hay rolls and turbines. The trailer park and the body shop. The baseball park and the junkyard. The small Greyhound station. My America, here, somewhere...

> *softly pronounces "nowhere"*

nowhere...in Nebraska. Can you let me go? Maybe.

> *sighs*

Weeds? Yes, yes I'll get to the weeds when I am finished doing the laundry, and, not to forget, cleaning the rooms. Yes, all the doors are opened. Airing out. If the grasshoppers get inside, in the sinks and the toilets, I'll be swiping and swatting at them with the Gideon Bible—again.

> *SHE takes a packet of Bubblicious gum that is wrapped up in the end of her dupatta. There is only one piece left. She takes it and chews. She tosses the wrapper in the basket.*

Enjoy yourself today. You're officially a week-old American. Yes, so am I. Well, I am off—I am off to the Whirlpool. The washer. Get out of the Jacuzzi and take a dip in the pool.

> *unenthusiastic*

Tootaloo.

> *A sigh—like the sigh before a cry. SHE picks up the basket and walks upstage. After a moment, she stops, turns around and looks into the audience—into town—into her America, nowhere. And then she exits. Blackout.*

END OF PLAY

Faith
Wm. P. Coyle

Cast
PRIEST — No younger than mid-30s

Time
The present

Setting
A funeral home

> *A wake. At the rear of the stage the corpse of an old woman lies in an open coffin. A few floral arrangements adorn the wall near the coffin or hang from stands. The PRIEST stands facing audience, holding a prayer book. The PRIEST has been speaking for a while before the action begins. In front of the PRIEST, with their backs to the audience, silhouetted in darkness, are four or five seated mourners. If actual people are not available, "people" props should suffice. Occasionally, a sniffle is heard from the mourners. When the PRIEST shifts to soliloquy, the mourners are shrouded in darkness. SOUND: Preferable, but not required, dirge music from an organ plays faintly in the background, up until the moment that we hear the PRIEST speaking. The PRIEST is fragile and continuously distracted throughout the service.*

PRIEST
And, so, that is why we are gathered here to say farewell to our beloved sister in Christ, Marion—

> *Polite whisper from a mourner: "Miriam"*

—Miriam...who joined Jesus and his Father in Heaven this past—

looks at his notes

—Wednesday, and has now been in Heaven with them for, oh, let's say about three days, in eternal life. And, though we are saddened by Marion's death, we are happy, too, for is this not really a celebration of her life?

> *LIGHTS OUT on mourners. Spotlight on PRIEST. The PRIEST begins a soliloquy. Each time PRIEST goes into soliloquy, lights out on mourners and spotlight on PRIEST.*

Celebration of her life! Jesus, that's pathetic. This bunch is just eating this stuff up, and I'm not even on today. I'm just burnt, that's it. Three of these a week for the past four months would drive anyone nuts...but how can I let them down? This is what they want to hear—that their loved one is in Heaven with Jesus. That Jesus is in Heaven. That there is a Heaven. A Jesus. That we'll meet Marion again in Heaven some day. That she'll just come walking up to us—no crutches, no walker, no leash to an oxygen tank—and introduce us to her bridge club. No dialysis. No adult diapers, no shit dripping down the backs of her legs. They want to know that she's a star now, a minor star in the other polity, not just another one gone off the cliff. They want to know because they'll be going her way soon. Especially that one, there, he looks like death warmed over. He might as well just stay here in the building, it won't be long for him. And look at her, old woman in all that silly makeup, hanging on my every word. What's her story? Widow? Big blue eyes. Seductive. She'd take me into the other room and go down on me if I could convince her everything will be alright. But I can't. Maybe the dumb ones. But even to them, I'm just a formality, a technicality, keeping them from the Yankee game. Who are they playing tonight, anyway? Boston. Or is it Baltimore?

> *LIGHTS UP on mourners.*

Um, for Jesus said, "My just man will live by faith, and if he draws back I take no pleasure in him." Her. My dear friends, Marion was not among those who draw back and perish, but among those who have faith and live.

points to corpse

So she is living right now, in Heaven, with our savior, though to you and me she looks dead.

hesitates

Yes, quite dead....

> *LIGHTS OUT on mourners. PRIEST looks at corpse*

Whoa. Really dead. I heard these people comment about how good she looks, how well they've dressed her up for this occasion. Well, people, I've got news for you: looks can be deceiving. I do fear the worst. Christ couldn't raise that lady if he used a crane. That's funny. OK, get it together, now...remember the prayers...say something about faith....

LIGHTS UP on mourners.

And though she is dead, she's not *really* dead. Death has no power over her, because she truly believed in our Lord, our Savior, Jesus Christ....

LIGHTS OUT on mourners.

I don't know this woman. I don't know her from Adam. Adam. Maybe I should get something about him in here somewhere. I don't know whether this woman truly believed. For all I know, she spent her days reading the Satanic Bible with a cucumber crammed up her ass. I don't know any of these people. I've never even seen them at my Mass.... Why did they ask me to do this?

LIGHTS UP on mourners.

And the Lord said unto Thomas, "You became a believer because you saw me. Blest are they who have not seen and have believed." Now, Marion—

> *One of the mourners clicks her tongue and whispers, loudly, "Miriam!"*

I'm sorry. Miriam—

LIGHTS OUT on mourners.

Marion, Miriam, what does it matter? She's dead. I'm sick of all these hostile bastards. What do they think, Miriam was the only person ever to die in this world? Look around, people, they're dying every day. And no one has figured it out yet. You people invite me here because you think I'm gonna make it all better: that I'm gonna chant a little hocus-pocus, and suddenly Miriam is sitting at the right hand of Christ, without that ugly little tumor on her head. Make you all feel better, less guilty for how you treated her when she was alive. Well, it's not that simple, folks.

> *gathering himself*

Well, I should remember her name at least. I guess that's not really too much to ask of me. Remember now, it's Marion, Marion—

LIGHTS UP on mourners.

—Marion—

Very loud tongue click from mourner.

—Miriam, no, Marion, no, Miriam...she never saw the Lord in her lifetime. Yet, if we have faith, we believe that she is now in Heaven with Christ— that she has been resurrected, and that we will be with her one day again, at the end of the world.

Audible yawn from a mourner. LIGHTS OUT on mourners.

End of the world. That's the first time I've really ever thought of that. What if the world doesn't end? What if science someday succeeds in keeping everyone alive forever. What about all those who have come before and died? What about me? What about Marion? Do we just...perish?

Another audible yawn from mourner

They're leaving. I guess they've heard enough. I've spoken too long. After all, what is there really to say? I suppose the game has begun, and their guilt and doubt miraculously assuaged. Ok, go now, get out of here...

LIGHTS UP on mourners.

Thank you. Thank you for coming. Go now, in the peace and love of our Lord Jesus Christ...

PRIEST stands for a few moments, watching the mourners leave. He turns to look at the corpse for a moment, looks forward again, then picks up a chair and carries it over to the casket. He sits in front of the casket, looking at the corpse. He pulls a flask from his vest pocket and takes a large gulp.

I guess they'll be coming for you soon. There should be more time. More time for us to think this out. Don't worry, though, I'll wait here with you. I'll wait here for a while. Here with you—

Takes a deep breath, and sighs; walks over to coffin, touches it gently and then speaks, confidently.

—Miriam.

END OF PLAY

The Librarian
Hugh Cardiff

The Librarian was produced at Knutsford Little Theatre, Knutsford, United Kingdom, October 2008, and performed by Ali Hulford.

═══════════════════════════════════════

Cast
MRS. MANNION — female, middle-aged

Time
Evenings, over a number of days

Setting
A library

Props
A keyboard, a table and chair, a telephone, a "Fines" box, white powder, and pills, armchair and lamp for sitting room, several hardback editions of Anna Karenina, several library books

Note
Ideally the stage should be dark, with the spot light on the librarian. The script can be adapted for a local setting, and cities and book titles may be changed, if required.

═══════════════════════════════════════

> The librarian, MRS. MANNION, is behind a table with a keyboard on it. She has reading glasses on, but looks out over them. She dresses drab and unfashionably. She is busy working away, and suddenly looks up.

MRS. MANNION

Oh, good evening. I didn't see you there. Welcome to Farnborough library. I hope you didn't have any trouble finding us. We're quite out of the way, aren't we? Tucked away, many miles from the highway. My name is Nora Mannion, and I'm the librarian here at Farnborough. The branch manager is Mr. O'Brien, but he only works days.

I've been here for over 20 years now. I joined the library service in 1975, worked in the big cities, Sheffield, Leeds, Manchester, did some time on the mobile libraries. Good fun for a young girl. But at some stage you have to settle down, and when I met Harold, we decided to make our life here, in a quiet country town. Away from the hustle and bustle.

smiles

A good environment for reading, no distractions.

starts typing, or sorting the books on her table, then holds up a book

Medicine for the soul.

puts book down

I've always maintained that the health of a society is reflected in the health of its libraries. And at Farnborough I think we're doing pretty well. Always room for improvement of course, but we have over 5,000 borrowers, or clients, as I like to call them. It is a business after all. If there was no-one borrowing books, we'd be shut down in the morning. We provide a vital service to the community. Not only is it a place of thought and creativity, it's also a place for some of our more senior clients to meet up. Loneliness can be a terrible thing.

Sometimes people ask me why I ever became a librarian. Apart from the obvious, my love of books, I like the the atmosphere in a library, that of learning and knowledge sharing. It's a stimulating environment, and I've been doing it so long now, I'm not really fit for anything else. When I started the ISBN, the International Standard Book Number, a great example of the international community working together, was only 10 digits, now it's up to 13. Just shows you how many books are out there. If there were no more books printed, you still wouldn't be able to read all the books currently published in one lifetime.

My role in the library is to handle customer queries, check books in and out, reserve books, and to handle newly arrived stock. Sometimes clients look for recommendations, so I usually have three or four stock responses to that. We now also have two computers on the Internet, so I'm in charge of the bookings and the tutorial courses we run for beginners.

Pause. LIGHTS change.

There was a complaint made today. Mr. O'Brien, the branch manager, sneaked up behind me, just when I was about to phone an overdue client, and said —

loud, in a man's voice

"Mrs. Mannion"

to audience, normal voice

—scared the life out of me. Says—

puts on male voice

"Do you know anything about the contents of *Kane and Abel*?" I turned around, and, calm as I could, said "Mr. O'Brien, you know I only read literature. Best sellers hold no interest for me." Jeffrey Archer, I mean, really.

puts on male voice

"Mrs Mannion, I am not referring to the printed matter, but rather, what was found inside the book."

shrugs shoulders

Quite bizarre. Mr. O'Brien refused to divulge who the complainant was, but what Mr. O'Brien doesn't know was that I remembered which clients last borrowed that book.

taps her forehead

Use it or lose it. I'll have a word with the client next time he's in, to get to the bottom of this. He's a bit of a busybody, to be honest with you.

SOUND: *phone rings. She picks it up.*

Farnborough Library.

pause

I'm afraid we don't have any copies of Anna Karenina in our branch.

pause

Well, we have ordered several copies in the past, but as soon as they're put on the shelf, they all seem to disappear

pause

I know, it's terrible. We do have *War and Peace*. That would keep you going for a while. Alternatively, you could try the county branch.

pause

Ok, thank you.

She puts phone down and gets ready to go home. She wraps scarf around her neck, puts on coat while speaking to audience.

We have implemented a new security scanner thing, which never works when it should. But you're always going to get books vanishing from time to time. It's human nature.

beat

I do have a story about *Anna Karenina*, but not a word to anyone else.

LIGHTS *fade.* MRS. MANNION *switches on a lamp. We are in her sitting room, she is sitting in an armchair, with a cup of tea, reading a copy of Anna Karenina, and beside her are several stolen hardback library copies of the book.*

"No furniture so charming as books."

indicating the books

Sydney Smith, 1771 to 1845.

It was a year last November, I was in the middle of *Anna Karenina*, totally engrossed in it. Tolstoy, what a genius. Anna was on her way to meet her lover Vronsky at the train station, when Harold suddenly says to me, out of the blue, "Nora, can I have a word?"

She pinches the remainder of the book she has to read, 100 pages or so and shows it to the audience, like she was showing it to Harold.

"Can it not wait?" I asked.

"No it can't", he said.

And that's when he lost the plot, and more words came tumbling out of his mouth in two minutes, than I'd heard in the previous two years. He was tired of living with a bookworm, he informed me. He was tired of the silence in the house, he was tired of me. And he had found someone else, he was leaving.

pause

I think it was Tolstoy that was the final straw. Maybe he thought that once I'd read all the English classics, that would be it. I would be free for him to do whatever he so wished, to dance attention on him and serve his every need, be at his beck and call. But when he saw me heading east, first with French books by Hugo and Marcel Proust, then the German Gunther Grasse, through Poland with the fabulous Milosz and on into Russia with Chekov, Turgenev, then Tolstoy. I think he must have thought there was no coming back for me. But what did he want me to do? Stop reading after Dickens?

pause, she sips cup of tea

Harold was a pharmacist, a dispenser of drugs. And he dispensed me.

pause

I...was dispensed with.

beat

It was difficult at first. Where love ends, hate begins. I had to stop myself from hating Harold, because hatred eats away at your soul. I turned to alcohol, then to prescription pills. At one stage Harold kept some painkillers about the place, so I had siphoned off a small amount. I'm not proud of it, but not ashamed of it either. I'm also a little superstitious, and I didn't want anyone else to go through what I went through. So I took all copies of Anna Karenina out of stock. As new copies arrived, I had to siphon them off too.

> *short snicker*

I didn't want *Anna* to be the cause of further marital difficulties. I still don't know what happened in the end, I cannot bring myself to finish it. I presume Anna and Count Vronsky lived happily ever after. But unfortunately life doesn't imitate fiction.

> *LIGHTS fade/change. She is back in Library, stacking books at the table. She is speaking to her side.*

Oh hello Mrs. Hunt, let me take those books off you.

> *takes a few books and checks them back in to stock, then hushed*

Now, there's £20 due on these please.

> *She reaches out into the dark and takes a £20 note, looks around her, is about to put the £20 into the Fines box, but then tucks it under her bra. She picks up a book.*

How did you like *Middlemarch*? Powerful stuff, hmmphh?

> *laughs, lifts another book*

I warned you. And *Fathers and Sons*? Not as much? Hmm, that's a surprise. Did you take them in order, like I said? *Fathers and Sons* first, then *Moby Dick*, then *Middlemarch*. In order of strength, with *Middlemarch* being the strongest.

> *beat*

Oh y'see, that's what happened. If you go from *Middlemarch* to *Fathers and Sons*, you're just not going to get that ...kick. Know what I mean?

> *LIGHTS change. MRS. MANNION is reading news paper. She looks up in shock*

Mrs. Coleman? I can't believe it. Found dead in her armchair —

> *reading from newspaper*

— "a library hardback edition of *The Mayor of Casterbridge* open on her lap."

> *looks up at audience*

And her only down last Thursday to borrow that very book.

> *reading from newspaper*

Her head was slumped to one side.

looking up

I know Hardy isn't the most exciting, but I've never heard of anyone who's died of boredom from it.

reading newspaper

"Police do not suspect foul play, however a prescription drug was found nearby, so they are awaiting the results of a toxicology report."

looking up

My God.

deep in thought for a moment, looks concerned

I wonder how I am going to get the book back.

types quickly on keyboard

Mrs. Weatherby has reserved it.

angry, stressed

You'd think she'd just go out and buy the bloody book. Her with her big bloody SUV.

beat, worried

Poor Mrs. Coleman, a lovely woman. Always paid on time, I mean, if she had any fines.

> *LIGHTS change. There is a long pause as MRS. MANNION looks out at audience*

I don't know what it is that people find uncomfortable about silence. If I had a penny for every time I've had to castigate a client for talking. It's not just kids, I can forgive them, but grown adults, some of whom seem to come in to the library just to chat.

shakes head

And Harold was obviously uncomfortable about it too. It's been a struggle without him, I'll admit that. I always expected him to be around. Well you do, don't you? Even if it's just to pay the bills. I was expecting to be able to retire off his pension and savings, but that option is now out the window. So I'll have to continue on working for a number of years, try and boost my savings, but a girl's gotta do what a girl's gotta do.

> *LIGHTS change. MRS. MANNION is on phone to police. She is irritated and stressed.*

Yes, you've already stated that officer, but it's not as if he was murdered by the book. It's not a weapon, so I don't understand why you won't return the book. It's not as if Hardy gave her a heart attack or whatever it was she died of. Yes...yes, I know. But we have a number of clients waiting to read that book....of course I'm not trying to obstruct the course of justice.

loses her temper

I'm just trying to get the bloody book back so that Mrs. Weatherby can borrow it.

slams the phone down

Suffering Jesus. You'd need the patience of a saint to deal with some people around here. Such ignorance.

LIGHTS change. MRS. MANNION holds up a flick-knife, and flicks it open. She then empties some white powder onto the table, and cuts it into segments with the knife, and gets it into a fine line. She takes a quick glance around, then snorts a little. The rest she pushes into a small plastic bag with a sealable zip.

"Some books are to be tasted, others to be swallowed, and some few to be chewed and digested." Francis Bacon. The writer, not the painter.

She then opens a library book, Three Men in a Boat, towards the end, and tapes the bag into back of book. She smoothes the bag, then closes the book. She then pops open a small bottle, and puts 2 or 3 pills into another plastic bag, opens Mrs.Chatterley's Lover, and tapes the bag into the back of the book.

Now Mrs. Thompson—

whispers

—allow at least 24 hours between *Three Men in a Boat* and *Mrs.Chatterley's Lover*, otherwise you may get the heebie-jeebies.

laughs

That will be £40, please, and thank you. Now, they're due back on the 5th.

pause

You do need to be discreet. I have a select group of clients that I provide this service for. People always go on about drugs, blah blah blah. Tobacco is a drug, alcohol is a drug. And if rosemary and thyme gave you any sort of kick, they'd probably classify them as drugs too. Well, let me tell you this, drugs helped me get over Harold. Nothing strong. Happy pills, I like to call them. And some of the people in this community have suffered too, either through bereavement, or their loved ones doing a Harold on them. Whatever. And I'm just helping them get through a difficult stage in their lives.

beat

I'll need to be careful though, especially after poor Mrs. Coleman. Not only does the medication give my clients a bit of a lift, it also enhances the reading experience for them, making it much more vivid. Sometimes they almost feel like they're living the life of the characters in the book, their imagination can run riot.

Usually, I conceal the consignment in parts of books people never read, just in case the client forgets to take the bloody stuff out, and returns it with the you-know-what still taped inside. What a hullabaloo that would be. Remember I was telling you about the *Kane and Abel* episode.

> *nods wisely*

That was Mr. Summerbee. Would forget his head if it wasn't screwed on. If there's a prologue, or footnotes at the back of a book, I usually tape them there, where most people wouldn't bother reading. So usually it's towards the back, or if it's Finnegan's Wake, anywhere after page 10 will do. No-one ever gets past the first 10 pages of that book.

> *She runs her finger along the table, to clean up up any remaining powder. She then looks dreamily to the side, into the distance, like she's looking out the window.*

Winter nights in the library are my favourite. With the winds and rains howling outside, watching the trees blow from side to side. What better place to be than huddled inside a building full of books.

> *beat*

The police rang. Want me to go down to the station—

> *makes apostrophe quotes with her fingers*

—"to answer some questions." Hmmmpph. I wonder what they want to ask me.

> *She looks dreamingly into distance, a little concerned. Then, after a pause:*

Anyway, no time for daydreaming, there are books to be checked in and forms to be filed.

> *She starts typing on keyboard as LIGHTS fade.*

> *END*

Night Vision
S. L. Daniels

Night Vision was a 2008 winner in the Theatre Oxford's Ten-Minute Play Contest and has been performed at the Powerhouse Community Arts Center in Oxford, Mississippi; the Newtown Theatre in Sydney, Australia, at the Short + Sweet Festival; the Gene Frankel Theatre in New York, (Endtimes Productions' Serling Award winner for Best Short Script); Circus Theatricals in Los Angeles for their 14th Annual Festival of New One-Act Plays; and Defector Art Theatre in Melbourne, Australia. It will be produced by Tympanic Theatre Company in Chicago in the fall.

Cast
ASHLEY — twenty or so, good-natured, bubbly

Time
Now

Setting
A small room with a dim lamp, a side table, and a bed

> *Night. Late. A small room with a dim lamp, a side table, and a bed. ASHLEY, 20-ish, stands in a short slip and ultra-high heels. She is good-natured, bubbly. Unflappably cheerful. <u>Never</u> self-pitying. Throughout the piece, she gradually wraps her body with gauze bandage.*

ASHLEY
I don't know what it is about the dark.

> *ASHLEY removes her left shoe and lifts her left leg onto a chair or side table. As she speaks, she begins to wrap her foot, then calf, then thigh in the gauze.*

The first time it happened, I was 14. I was having sex with my Uncle Danny.

Okay, hold up. I know what you're thinking: Typical. Innocent kid molested by her skeevy old uncle.

It wasn't like that. Maybe *I* molested *him*. My Uncle Danny is majorly cool. And he is not old.

He had just gotten back from prison—a *total* mix-up. Some unfair meth charge. His friend knew this guy who was a nurse. And needed to get what Danny thought was medication to a hospital...

Or something.

So anyway. He gets back from prison. It's night. And he looks all sad. And pale. And, I don't know. Hungry.

I am jumping all over him. *So* excited he's back!

He's like: "Get off of me, douche!" "Quit trying to kiss me, skank." "Dude, what are you, *desperate?*"

But then he tilts his head. Taps his finger on his chin. Looks deep into the air, like a mad scientist getting an idea.

> *ASHLEY finishes wrapping her left leg, and puts her bandaged foot back into her shoe. As she speaks, she begins to wrap her right leg, then foot, then calf, then thigh.*

Next thing I know, he throws me over his shoulder, charges up the stairs.
> *with admiration*

He is *so strong*.

I bet he could tear a door off its frame.

I bet he could lift an Ultimate Fighter with each arm.

I bet he could bash through the brick wall of a 7-11.

So we're in my grandmother's bedroom, and he tosses me on the bed, like he'd toss a body into a grave or something. Just random, you know? My nose lands on the old bedspread. It smells like detergent and marshmallows.

Danny's pulling his clothes off, my clothes off.

I don't know *what's* going on!

It's dark. Just a thread of light from the hallway.

> *ASHLEY places her right foot back into her shoe. She begins to wrap her left hand, and left arm.*

Danny presses my shoulders down. I can barely see his skin. Right as he's over me, right as he's on top of me—

His face.

In the dark.

The grey glow of light on the outline of his features.

I swear.

He morphs. Right as I'm looking up at him. In the almost dark.

He starts off as Danny.

The Danny who told me that eating live ants would make me grow taller. The Danny who dared me to drink a whole can of beer when I was eight. And laughed when I puked all over his shorts. It *was* funny.

It's Danny's face.

But then . . . it's *Dracula's* face. From the old Dracula movies my grandmother used to make me watch with her.

It's still Danny. But Danny is *Dracula*. The shadows. The light. I don't know why.

His side teeth look long and sharp.

His hairline points on his forehead.

His eyes look through me like I'm nourishment and nothing more....

> *ASHLEY begins to wrap her right hand and right arm—the hand is wrapped a little loosely so that she has adequate dexterity for the remaining wrapping.*

So okay. *Dracula* is on top of me, about to do me, and I'm lying there thinking, "How could Danny be a vampire all these years, and I didn't know it?"

It doesn't make sense. I've seen him awake during the day. A ton. I've seen him eat garlic. On like, *everything*. Holy crap, I've even seen him in church once or twice.

This *can't* be Dracula.

But I look up. As he's rocking above me. Making noises like he's trying to lift something heavy. And there he is, sure as blood:

Dracula›

After it's done, I run to turn on the light. *I have to see.*

It's Danny again.

Same old Danny. Who says if I tell anyone, he'll smother me with my pillow next time I go to sleep.

But he's just *posing*, acting tough. All stressing about going back to prison for me being a minor. But it's only 8 years different.

Him at 22, me at 14. Not much older. If you take, like, *all* of time. You know, eternity. I bet 8 years is like a second.

> *ASHLEY begins to wrap the bottom of her torso, and works her way up to her waist, then chest, as she speaks.*

I didn't have sex for a while after that first time. Danny got a girlfriend. And I didn't want any more nocturnal encounters with Nosferatu, if you know what I mean.

But then, the next guy? My third year in high school? Same thing happened.

Or kind of.

Kirk. On the weight-lifting team. Everyone said he was mean, but they just didn't get him. It was the *steroids. He had to take them for the sake of his team.*

So we're doing it in his mom's mini-van. In the middle of this dark parking lot. Deserted. And you can pretty much guess what happens.

Kirk sets me down across the arm rest. Climbs on top of me. Next thing I know, it's the Incredible Hulk. Not Dracula. The *Hulk.*

Greenish skin.

Block neck.

Fierce glassy eyes.

It is *weird!*

I end it with Kirk the next day. He breaks my rib, gets sent to juvie. That was that.

But not really. Cause since then? It keeps happening.

I see different things. Different, you know. Freaky-type beings. Almost every time I'm with a guy.

In that way.

In the dark.

So okay, since it started, I've done:

A Werewolf.

A Frankenstein.

A Jason.

A Chucky. The doll AND his bride.

2 Freddy Kruegers.

Pennywise the Clown.

Candyman.

Michael Myers. Not the Austin Powers dude and his mini-him, although that *could* happen, almost. The Halloween murderer.

Couple demons from Buffy.

Ghostface.

Leatherface.

Tallman.

Pinhead.

And Leprechaun. The evil one. With the stunted torso and high-buckled shoes. Who pogo-sticked on a guy's chest? Leprechaun. Blechhh!

Every time it happens, I want to run out of the room screaming. Like a spazz in a horror movie. But I just lie there. My heart beating in my teeth.

ASHLEY begins to wrap her shoulders and neck.

One guy I did, he was *so* fine-looking! Samuel. So beautiful.

Long dark hair in his eyes. Snow white skin. I thought for sure he couldn't turn into something bad.

But wouldn't you know. Lights off. He's on me. And with his delicate face and hair, suddenly he's the creepy little girl from "The Ring." Samara. (Shivers) She is not cute at all.

ASHLEY carefully begins to wrap her face and head — chin to crown, cheeks, nose, forehead. She leaves an opening for her mouth, and slits for her eyes.

Anyway, it all, you know, really puts a damper on the whole sex thing. Which is my *job*. So it pretty much puts a damper on my whole life.

But last year? I remembered this other old movie. There was this wrapped-up zombie thing? And *nobody* could harm it. *It was already dead!!*

I know it'll seem a little strange at first. But most guys say they like it. They come back!

wraps

You can do anything you want.

wraps

And you can have the lights on or off.

wraps

If you do turn them off?

leans forward

I can tell you what kind of scary creature you are.

ASHLEY secures the last end of bandage across her face. Fully welcoming — and fully wrapped — she holds out her open arms.

END

A Slight Limp—The Later Life and Adventures of Tiny Tim
Steven Korbar

A Slight Limp... premiered in December 2004 at the Palos Verdes Players in Torrance, California, along with its companion piece *A Brief Moment for Our Jewish Friends or Ernie Ackerman Explains the Hanukkah Bush*. It was directed by Charles Bates, featured the playwright as Timothy and the stage manager was David Meyers.

Cast
TIMOTHY B. CRATCHIT

Time
An evening around Christmas

Setting
A stage

> *A man in Dickensian-era clothing walks across the stage, displaying a slight limp as he moves along. Just as he is about to exit, he stops, seems to fight for his composure, then turns, paranoiac and angry, and addresses the audience in a thick Cockney accent.*

TIMOTHY

Alright, what are you looking at me like that for! I'm not bothering anyone. I'm only walking here. Nothing unusual about that, nothing out of hand. Oh perhaps I haven't got the chipperest of gaits, so what? Maybe I've got a pebble in me shoe. Perhaps I'm just tired from me work...long day at the Industrial Revolution. But no, you don't believe that, do you? Sitting there staring at me like I was Queen Victoria about to pull sixpence out of me bum. Oh I've seen your type before. Think you recognize me, do ya? All at once craving a few choruses of "Good King Wenceslas?" Having the sudden, unexplainable urge to make merry with a big stuffed goose at the very sight of me!? Well alright then, alright; not going to be satisfied till you know for sure? Well then, let's have this done here and now. I'm not ashamed, I've done nothing wrong. You want to know the truth, well I'll tell you then, I'll tell you who I am and a humbug to all these noisy, prying inquisitions...

stepping forward defiantly

I am Timothy B. Cratchit Esquire...DON'T CALL ME TINY.

Are you surprised, disappointed, not what you were expecting? Well join the cold, hard world; I hit a growth spurt. You wouldn't even have given me a second look if it wasn't for the limp, would you? It always gives me away. It's not even a bad limp; but if you were in my irregular-sized boots you would know that sometimes the small ones are worst. You would understand that having a slight limp is akin to being a castrated sex-fiend: you retain all of the shame but receive none of the benefits.

At least in the old days, when I was clumping along like an ompah band, people would throw coins at me in the streets. But now all it's good for is affording the masses one final opportunity to make me feel as if I've somehow let them down by growing up. David Copperfield you let age gracefully. Oliver Twist falls in with a gang of cutthroats and eventually drifts into male prostitution; nobody raises an eyebrow. But me, oh no, I'm supposed to remain unchangingly wistful, forever young and vulnerable, perpetually...tiny. This is an adjective applied much more advantageously to a six-year-old boy than it is to a fully-grown man, if you know what I mean. I swear by the holy Church of England, if I have to listen to one more snide witticism about my Fezziwig, I am going to take a human life.

Just imagine what it's been like for me all these years. Strangers walking up to me and saying, right to me face, such things as, "Didn't you used to be..." or "We just loved you when you were little" and of course, "Come on then, be a good bloke and let us take a peek at the withered leg." Now and again I'll even get one of those freaky buggers come up to me with a gamy glint in his eye and ask me if he can "touch me stump." Bit of the Oscar Wilde crowd if you catch me drift. But that's not even the worst of it, no, there is one humiliation that's more horrendous than all the others rolled together. One soul crushing ritual that has been the bane of me tortured existence; the one inevitable moment when some thoughtless dunderhead walks up to me and feverishly demands that I say...IT.

looking at the audience with hostility

Oh don't play coy with me; you know what I'm talking about! Bloody hell, I said it once when I was six years old! How would you like it if people came up and asked you to repeat, "Look mummy, I made a right proper boom-boom," you wouldn't! Yet everyday I hear, "Say it." "Come on, just say it." "Say it to me kids." "Say it to me dog." "Say it too me dottering old mum." Alright, I'll say it if you'll just leave me peace…one last time before they cart me off to Bedlam…. "God bless us all, everyone." I've been asked to say that more times than a tart's asked directions to the fleet.

Maybe it wouldn't be so bad if people could at least get the saying right, but I'm constantly getting requests for things like "God bless everybody all the time." But wait, it gets even balmier, sometimes they ask me for, "Please sir, can I have some more." "It is a far, far better thing I do." "Out damn spot!" "Oh Heathcliff! I'll meet you in the Heather." and occasionally even, "Looky there, Gretel! I think I sees me a gingerbread house!" Bloody uneducated dolts. And you know, if you really want to get the quote correct, what I actually said was, "God bless us, everyone." No "all." I was referring only to members of me immediate family, and if I recall properly, at the time I was excluding my older brother Peter, as he was a bit of a git and had the habit of repeatedly tying me in a flour sack and trying to throw me into the Thames.

a nostalgic little laugh

Oh that Petey. What a scamp he was, what a rascal. Those were the days; back before fame came and ruined everything. It's true things were tough, we weren't wealthy or important; in fact we were destitute and diseased, but we didn't care. We had each other. There were eight of us jolly Cratchit children—not counting the thirteen that died in infancy—and oh the fun we would have together. Nothing so grand, just the normal things that everybody does. Taking long family rides in the country and mum making a game of which one of us kids could point out the most Syphilitics along the road. Me brothers and me coming up with new and less sanitary ways of lighting the Christmas pudding, and of course, all us boys walking into the grocers and asking the shopkeeper if he had "Prince Albert in a can"…yes well, we always seemed to get caught at that one, didn't we? But still such fun.

But me very happiest recollections of this very happy time are, without a doubt, of my Dad. Never has a grown man loved a little boy better than my dad loved his Tiny Tim.

eyeing audience critically

Now don't go smutting that up into something dirty. It was always said that Bob Cratchit treated all his children as good as gold, but everyone knew that he had a special place in his heart for me. Maybe it was the timidness in me eyes, or the mildness of me voice, or maybe it was the fact that I had the life expectancy of an amoeba. But no matter, my Dad couldn't do enough for me, he would feed me, bathe me, and carry me about the streets of London perched high upon his shoulders...and these were the days when incontinence was still a problem for me. But my Dad didn't mind. Indeed, the only shadow over our happiness at this time was that of my continued lameness. Me father just couldn't understand why I had to be the one that was stricken; putting aside the knowledge that, due to our wretched poverty, I had, by the age of five contracted —

reeling them off

measles, mumps, whopping cough, typhoid, yellow fever, diphtheria, head lice, infectious hepatitis, and an extremely stubborn bout of tropical malaria, although where I picked that one up none of us was quite sure. But still, my Dad always kept the hope in his heart that someday, the blessing of health he prayed so fervently for on my behalf would somehow come to pass.

How could we ever have guessed that that day would arrive, like a perforating sprig of holly through our unsuspecting hearts. December the 25th, 1843, when a cheap, gibbering old man sent us the gift of anonymous poultry and changed our lives forever. You've all heard the story...unless you've been living in a wine vat. Suffice to say that this was the arrival of me famous benefactor, the newly repentant Mr. Ebenezer Scrooge, whose name had previously struck fear in all and had always sounded to me brothers and me like an act of fornication permanently prohibited by Scotland Yard. Now, me only previous experience with this terrifying man had been through infrequent, chance meetings as my Dad carried me about the streets, where Mr. Scrooge's uncharitable demeanor would find me repeatedly expressing me unbridled terror down the back of me fathers neck. And yet, here was this same gargoyle, merry as you please, promising to better all our lives, find me the finest of medical care and, commencing the day after Christmas, to up my Dad fifteen bob a week. I didn't like the sound of this last part one bit. In fact, all of us thought the odious old crank had gone completely balmy.

But my Mother, being a good Christian woman, reminded us all that upon this day a savior had been born. And that this holy child would surely ask us, with open arms, to welcome this lonely old man into the bosom of our loving family. She also pointed out that Mr. Scrooge was very, very rich. As she put it later privately, if the loony old Nutball wants to throw away his gold, he might as well aim it directly at our pockets. We never really did fully understand Mr. Scrooge's complete change of character, although as you probably remember he always claimed it had to do with a visitation from three ghosts. Members of me family, however, somewhat doubt this pronouncement as over the ensuing years he also claimed to see goblins, ghouls, zombies, trolls, creatures from outer space, assorted Yeti, and the spirit of Elizabeth the First having unnatural relations with Mary, Queen of Scots in a pickle barrel.

Still, it is true that over time it was said that Mr. Scrooge became like a second father to me. Interestingly, I always looked upon him as much more of an elder brother; particularly after he eventually married me fourteen-year-old sister Emily; decency laws being a good deal less stringent back then. I found the whole arrangement rather dicey meself, but as my mother said to my hysterical sister upon her wedding day, Mr. Scrooge was very, very rich. Yet in his stated promise to help me overcome me pitiable lameness, old Scrooge was as good as his word and better.

And slowly, in time, the bloom did start coming back into me cheeks. I began to walk with more strength and sureness everyday.

Oh sure, there were the occasional setbacks, a slight case of influenza...strep throat, pneumonia, scarlet fever, cholera, dropsy, the grip, tetanus, jungle rot, pink eye, rheumatic fever, tuberculoses of the bone and joint; and an unidentified series of complaints that me wiseacre brothers tried to convince me were actually female troubles. But my bum leg was feeling stronger all the time.

News of my astonishing recovery spread like pestilence across the countryside. People came from miles around just to gaze upon my rosiness and marvel. Eventually, with the spontaneous contributions people would make, and the tax-exempt foundation me mother set up in my name, the day came when we didn't even need Mr. Scrooge's benevolent financial support anymore, although we took it just the same. As me good old mum put it, we were raking it in hand over fist. I was a sensation! For a while there was even some talk that I was the recipient of a miracle. That perhaps the Saints had intervened on my behalf. But me family decided to play down this aspect of the story after weeks on end of being beaten senseless by Protestants in our neighborhood. The most unfathomable aspect of these attacks being that we were ourselves Protestants. But despite those few drawbacks to me popularity, it seemed that the sun had finally shown on us woebegone Cratchits. I was now famous, beloved, known far and wide as everyone's favorite son. And the brilliant part was, it all came so effortlessly. Simply assuring us that happiness was a thing that arrived, as if over night...and so is how we took it, for a very long and happy time.

And then one day, some years later, as I was nearing the age of thirteen, I felt something different. At first I just naturally assumed it was Meningitis, but it wasn't. It was something else. I felt a stirring inside of me. I began to change and grow...and grow...and GROW!! Sweet Jesus, it wouldn't stop!!

It was as if savage nature was overcompensating for me former pathetic puniness. Overnight me britches suddenly displayed a good six inches of naked calf. Hair started sprouting in places it oughtn't, and unspeakable parts of me suddenly grew altogether murky and disagreeable. It was a hellish nightmare. Mum tried desperately to reconfigure me little waistcoats and Dad had more and more difficulty hoisting me upon his shoulders, his final fruitless effort causing the good man three ruptured vertebrae.

And then the day arrived. Someone spotted me. There was the usual recognition, the inevitable request and my customary gracious acquiescence in saying for me dotting admirers..."God bless us all..."
        voice cracking and dropping an octave
"everyone." It just didn't have the same effect anymore.

Things quickly went down hill from there. People just didn't want to deal with me in this new and bloated form. They all looked at me as if I betrayed them. As if somehow they wanted their pity back. All at once donations began to dry up. There were problems with the bookkeeping. One of me brothers ended up serving time in the workhouse and another at a penal colony in Australia. Mum felt genuinely grieved testifying against them both. And certainly it wouldn't do to ask Mr. Scrooge for additional funds, especially since, by this point he had divorced my sister to marry a younger woman. I became despondent and took to me bed. I just couldn't understand how everyone could desert me like this. I felt as if I would never want to leave my little abode again. Until the morning me Mum came into me room, leaned over to where I was lying and said something to me that would change me life forever... "You're big as a bloody Ox now, get the hell out of my blinking house!" That day I left the place of me birth with nothing more than I had entered into it with, except for a near-to-breaking heart.

And so began me days of exile. I traveled around the countryside, aimlessly trying to find some meaning in it all. It seemed so pointless now, as if I were just going around in circles; a feeling probably compounded by the fact that I always just naturally tend to veer to the left anyway.

After a brief stint in Her Majesty's Royal Navy—where my official rank was ballast—I ventured from city to town trying desperately to lose meself in the populous, stopping only once to briefly recover from a very slight case of bursitis…complicated by anemia, jaundice, epilepsy, trench mouth, black lung, black death, red death, typhoid again, shingles, rabies, anaphylactic shock, hysterical blindness, and an unbelievably nasty case of swimmer's ear! Oddly, in a strange Anglophilic irony, all my life I've always had perfect teeth

Still, it was only a brief respite in me unhappy odyssey. Part of me just wanted to disappear; it's hard enough to find your place in this world when all your life you've gotten by by being sickly and adorable, but the burden of past fame makes the search seem unbearable. I tried to disguise meself, to be anonymous, but always this cursed limp would give me away. On days when the weather would turn foul, my leg would stiffen and the clumpity-clump would grow so noticeable I'd become self-conscious and be forced to use a crutch to avoid all the prying, unwanted attention.

> *HE pulls out a tiny child's crutch, clearly the famous one from "A Christmas Carol."*

People seemed to recognize me all the same.

Yet, admittedly, these brushes with fame did make me realize that there existed another part of me that missed the limelight. Oh I know, it's an old cliché, the former child star trying to recapture his past glory, but I did need funds badly, and I always rather fancied the idea of a life upon the stage: a season with the Old Vic, a command performance before Her Majesty. And in time I did find myself a position with what you might call a…band of roving players. You also might call it a carnival. To be specific, "Colonel Willy's Famous Flea Circus and Astonishing Freak Museum."

Not what I was hoping for, not what I was used to. Once I had been beloved by the whole of England and now I was brushing aside chicken feathers from the geeks at a broken down sideshow. What's worse, I wasn't even the star attraction of the proceedings. I received but fourth billing in the freak show line up…and since one of the acts ahead of me were Siamese Twins; fifth really! The humiliation became too much for me. The sight of all those midgets and dwarfs only made me realize all the happiness I had lost. By the second year I became so depressed even the pinheads couldn't make me laugh anymore. But the final mortification came the day a particularly bitter hermaphrodite spitefully supplied me with the knowledge that I was being paid but half the wages of "Bucky the Dog-faced Boy." And in Bucky's case, management was throwing in scraps off the table as well.

That was the end. I just couldn't take it anymore. It was this last humiliation that led me to the bleakest point in me life. I speak of it now only that others may learn from my misfortune and avoid the wretched and depraved fate that I succumbed to. If you take away nothing else from hearing of my experiences, I beg of you heed this warning of a deadly and pervasive threat to our precious, modern youth. Kids, whatever you do...STAY AWAY FROM OPIUM DENS. It's not the answer. You only think you're walking without a limp. What you're really doing is heading strait for the vortex that leads you directly to the sewers of London, and in case you haven't been there lately, let me tell you, it doesn't smell like a custard fresh out of the oven down there!

But that's where I ended up—the lowest of the low. It seemed my story had reached its final chapter. That destiny had chosen for me this sad and sorriest of epilogues. And yet, as I have come to know over time, many an ending is merely the precipice from which to view a new and more promising road. And that, unlike Mr. Dickens, the Good Lord has never had to worry about plot credibility when it comes time for settling our fates. For here it was, at the nadir of my life, that I suddenly found its most precious jewel. I still blush at the very thought of it...the day I met my future bride. Yes, there she was, as if waiting for me like a delicate flower. A sweet and lovely morphine addict named Maribell. I noticed her right away...lying in the gutter next to me. I swear it was love at first sight. We had so much in common, our appreciation of music, our love of the countryside, the tiny animals we imagined running up and down the walls. But best of all from my view of things, being that Maribell was completely illiterate, she had never even heard of me. I was just her Timothy, and that was enough. She became my intended and, after mutually committing ourselves to hospital, where we were stripped, shaved, and thrown yowling into the snake pit, we were married.

And from that point on all things seemed possible again. I know it's an old saying, but true: All a good man needs to succeed is a good women and former dope-fiend behind him. Even my financial fortunes reversed themselves in time.

After searching far and wide I finally found a new profession that suited me perfectly...I began selling life insurance. Door-to-door at first, but me record became so impressive, only three claims paid in twelve months and that was in a plague year, I was eventually kicked upstairs...where I have become a pioneer in the new and exciting field of personal health insurance and where, based upon me past medical history, Lloyds of London has recently coined a new phrase in my personal honor: Preexisting Condition!

No man could have asked for more blessings than had been heaped upon me. I had seemingly found the contentment you all believed was predestined for me in the story. But it wasn't what I saw; I had had to go out and find it for meself. And I couldn't understand why it had taken so long, what the purpose was of all the pain and wasted time I had endured to reach this place.

And then one day, not so very long ago, I received a post from me father, bidding me come home. It seemed old Mr. Scrooge had finally died and requested that I attend his service. As I stood in the church alone with me Mother and Father...most of me heartier brothers and sisters having died by then,

a little gloating laugh

I looked upon me benefactor's face one final time, and I couldn't help but reflect on all the misery he had unintentionally caused me and I'm ashamed to say I could not find it in me heart to forgive him. I couldn't wish him peace, as I had still never truly found it meself.

That night, I slept in me father's house one last time, in me old room, in me old bed, and I had, of all things, a strange dream. In it a phantom appeared to me and showed me scenes of things that were and would yet be. Of people and places of the past and future, only I was nowhere among them. All there was to suggest that I had ever walked upon this Earth was a vacant seat in the poor chimney corner. And a crutch without an owner...carefully preserved. And then the phantom led me to a lonely place and pointed an empty sleeve at a single gravestone and upon the marker read the words... "Tiny Tim."

beat, then becoming incensed

...Not even a last name! Just bloody Tiny Tim. And I swear, and I'm not just being over sensitive, but the "Tiny" was in a slightly bolder print than the "Tim".

So there it was, for all blinking eternity, and finally, belatedly, I understood the real meaning of the gift that Mr. Scrooge had given me. Simply, the opportunity to make a name for meself in the world. I had had to learn that, storybooks to the contrary, happily-ever-after is not something that's just presented to you as if by spectral hands. You don't discover that in the confines of one haunted night, but rather every day in the broad light of morning, and again the next day, and the next. The value of it being as much in the striving as it is in the prize itself. Every man's life must have its struggles. Its striding success, its limping failure. Its moments of pure and surpassing joyousness...and its Fezziwig jokes. And with that thought in my head, I felt ready, at long last, to lift my glass and say, "To Mr. Scrooge, the founder of the feast."

And at that, freed at last, I left me fathers house and set out, irregular gait and all, back to me own home. To me loving wife, me lucrative career in insurance, and to the proudest reason any man may find to look forward to the future bravely...a son of me very own: Timothy B. Cratchit, Jr. The strongest, healthiest boy ever to set foot on the streets of merry old London...you hardly even notice the rickets. May that truly be said of us all.

And so, as someone much younger, though wiser, once adorably observed, so many Yuletides ago..."A merry Christmas to all...and to all a bleedin' goodnight!'

> *HE turns to exit, then stops a moment, reconsiders and turns back to the audience good-naturedly.*

...Oh what the bloody hell, you paid your quid..."God bless us all, everyone!"

> *HE gives a jaunty little wave to the audience and limps off stage to the tune of "Here We Come A Caroling," as LIGHTS fade.*

END OF PLAY

10-Minute Plays

All The Way
Steven Korbar

All the Way premiered in January 2007 as part of "Pick of the Vine" at Little Fish Theatre in San Pedro, California. It was directed by Erich Whitaker and featured Andy Kallok and Kacy Peacock. In 2008 it was produced as part of *Reservations for Two* at Write/Act Repertory in Los Angeles, directed by Daniel T. Green and featuring Jack Seal and Alana Dietze. It also won Third Place in the Camino Real Playhouse ShowOff! International Playwriting Festival in 2007-2008.

Cast of Characters
SYD — a man of about 70
LYNN — a young woman in her 20s

Time
Early evening

Setting
A hotel room

> *In a hotel room setting, SYD, a man of about 70 is pacing nervously. He is a rather average looking man, but there is a tenseness to him that makes him seem unpredictable and menacing. After a time there is a knock on the door. SYD freezes for a moment but then moves to answer it. At the door is LYNN, an attractive young woman in her 20s. Her manner is controlled, professional; almost excessively self-possessed.*

       SYD
Yes?

       LYNN
Hi. I'm Lynn. I think you've been expecting me?

SYD
> *rather hurriedly ushering her in*

Yes.

LYNN

I know I'm a few minutes late; I'm sorry. I hope you weren't waiting long.

SYD
> *nervously*

No.

LYNN

It's just amazing what a little rain does to the drivers in this city. It's like they can't figure out what all this wet stuff falling on their windshields is.

SYD
> *abruptly handing her an envelope*

Here's your money...
> *awkwardly*

They told me I had to pay you right when you got here.

LYNN
> *in control*

Well thank you. I hope I can take your eagerness as a compliment.

SYD

They told me to pay you when you first got here.

LYNN
> *taking the envelope*

Is it alright if I take off my coat?

SYD

Sure.

turning away slightly

LYNN
Thank you.

> *Removing her coat, we see that she is wearing a stylish, expensive looking dress.*

SYD
> *a beat, then tensely*
...Did they tell you I was...older?

LYNN
Of course. They know I prefer spending time with mature gentlemen. Would you like to tell me your name?

SYD
> *uncertain*
Could I not?

LYNN
That's fine. A little mystery can be fun.

SYD
You don't have to tell me your name either...
> *awkwardly*
I know you already did, but...

LYNN
...Forget it.

SYD
> *very nervous*
I put the amount they told me in the envelope, all of it. Now for that, you're going to do what ever I tell you, right?

LYNN

For that amount you and I are going to have a wonderful evening together.

SYD

And you'll do whatever I want?

LYNN

I don't think there's anything you're going to ask for that I can't give you.
seductively
Would you like to start by watching me undress?

SYD

turning away sharply, speaking with difficulty
I want...something special.

LYNN

stopping, careful
That's okay. Did you mention what you'd like when you called?

SYD

No.

LYNN

Well that can kind of change the amount that I'll need to ask you for.

SYD

How much more?

LYNN

It depends.

SYD

reaching for his wallet
Why don't I just give you some money and...

LYNN
I need to know what it is first or I can't go ahead.

SYD
ashamed
What if it really isn't...regular?

LYNN
delicately
That might be alright. I'm not delicate; nothing you say is going to shock me.

SYD
You're thinking I'm some sort of freak, aren't you?

LYNN
calmly
I'm not here to think.

SYD
What if I give you double what I already paid?

LYNN
slight pause
...You must have something interesting in mind.

SYD
I'll give you double and I won't mention it to the people you work for.

LYNN
interested, considering
...Ever?

SYD
But then you have to do whatever I tell you.

LYNN

You keep saying that. Are you trying to scare me? Because if you want, I can be scared for you.

SYD
getting out his wallet
I'll give you the extra money right now.

LYNN

Are you thinking you want to be rough with me; is that it? Because if that's what you're looking for, I don't have a problem with it. You're not going to hurt me.

SYD
not acknowledging what she has said
Here...
handing her the money

LYNN
slight pause, then gingerly
...Okay
taking the money
...It's a deal. Neither one of us wants what we do to leave the room; and this way we both know it never can. And so long as we don't get too loud,
a subtle warning
because you know, if I yelled or something, someone would come, so long as that doesn't happen, you can do what ever you want. Just tell me what it is.

SYD seems suddenly paralyzed for a moment, unsure what to do, but then slowly walks across the room.

Should I come, too?

SYD
No.

LYNN
Okay.

SYD
> *stopping*

Don't look at me like that.

LYNN

I'm not...looking.

> *SYD retrieves an old suitcase, puts it on a chair and unzips it.*
> *He is about to open it, but then stops with a disturbing thought.*
> *Looking at LYNN.*

SYD
> *uneasily, not knowing how to express himself*

Have you...I have to ask if you've...washed.

LYNN

...What?

SYD

Have you washed...since the last time you did this? You have to be very clean.

LYNN
> *taken aback, not knowing what to say*

...I...

SYD

Have you?

LYNN
> *a bit terse*

Yes.

> *After a moment, Syd slowly pulls a dress from the suitcase. The*
> *dress is formal, a party dress circa late 1950s. He holds it up for*
> *a moment, displaying it, as if hoping that Lynn will naturally*
> *know what to do.*

LYNN
> *a long beat, comically uncertain*

...Now, did you want me to put that on, or were you planning on—

SYD
> *shocked*

No! You.

LYNN

I just want to be sure. I'll be happy to put it on. I can't guarantee it will fit...

SYD

It should, I asked for someone your size.

LYNN
> *a bit disturbed by what SYD has said*

Oh.

> *LYNN walks to SYD and takes the dress. She turns and offers to let him unzip her.*

Do you want to help me...

SYD
> *walking away*

Just change into it.

LYNN
> *beginning to change, looking at the dress*

It's very pretty.
> *slightly apprehensive, then smiling*

I'm going to feel just like Doris Day.

SYD

I know it's not very fashionable.

LYNN
Sort of a retro look.

SYD
not looking at her, mostly to himself
Styles change I suppose. I didn't really think about that. Ladies notice that kind of thing more than men. I guess it's all pretty much the same to us. Then one day you see an old picture or a movie or something and you suddenly realize how different everybody looks; and it kind of catches you off guard, just doesn't seem right somehow. Women are more prepared for that I guess; they keep track of those things better.

LYNN
now dressed, quietly
Okay, I'm ready.
showing the dress a bit, then indicating her hands
The only thing I'm missing is a pair of those funky little white...
SYD is now staring at LYNN, almost stricken.
...What?
Frozen, SYD does not answer.
...Do you want me to get into bed?

SYD
flatly
No.

LYNN
taking the initiative, walking to SYD provocatively
Maybe you'd like me to give you a little help? Maybe I could sort of start you off and...
She reaches to unbuckle Syd's belt.

SYD
pulls back, strongly
...Stop it!

LYNN
unnerved
Then what do you want me to do?

After a moment, SYD tentatively moves back to his suitcase. He looks in it and then begins scanning the room in search of something.

What are you looking for?

SYD
An outlet.

LYNN
alarmed
Oh crap?!

SYD
Oh, no. I think it works without it.

Pulling out a small CD player and setting it on top of the suitcase, SYD begins to fiddle with it, trying to get it to play but is unable, preoccupied.

My grandson tried to show me how to use this.
trying again
Oh, wait! There.

The CD begins to play Frank Sinatra singing "All the Way." SYD seems pleased for a moment, but then turns to LYNN and again appears uncertain. They stare at each other for a time until SYD finally musters a shaky resolve, moves to LYNN and holds out his arms in an invitation to dance, she is apprehensive.

...Please.

LYNN
a kind of dread
...I don't dance very well.

SYD
...It's what I want.

> *SYD keeps his arms stretched and, hesitantly, LYNN joins him.*
> *They begin to sway awkwardly. There is a silence.*

LYNN
> *quietly*
...This is like, a Frank Sinatra song, right?

SYD
> *acknowledging*

Mmm.

LYNN
From a long time ago.

SYD
Yes.
> *a smile*

1957.

> *Short silence.*

LYNN
I'll just let you tell me what you want to do next.

SYD
> *quietly*
...Just this.

LYNN
...Don't you think you'd enjoy it if I—

SYD
No...

LYNN
> *a beat, then conceding softly, as if she already knew the answer*

...No.

> *There is a short silence as LYNN thinks a moment.*

I'll give you back the extra money.

SYD

Thank you.

> *There is a longer silence.*

LYNN
> *hesitantly*

...You danced to this with somebody?

> *SYD considers if he should answer; then nods his head 'yes.'*

And this was hers?

> *meaning the dress*

Is she...do you know where she is now?

SYD
> *a beat, than simply*

About ten minutes from our house. She doesn't recognize me most days. We'll have our 47th in March.

LYNN
> *trying to comprehend, almost hurt*

...All those years...just one woman?

SYD
> *softly*

...Just one.

LYNN
> *a beat, shaking her head in quite awe*

...Shit.

There is a short silence. They stumble a bit in their dancing. LYNN is rattled.

I'm sorry. I told you I wasn't any good at this.

SYD
You're fine.

LYNN
You should have told them what you wanted me for. I don't like to get involved in this kind of thing. I'm not comfortable.
a certain irony
...It's just such a waste of my abilities. Are you really sure you wouldn't rather knock me around a little? Tie me up; maybe violate me with a foreign object? I swear, you can't hurt me.

SYD reaches out his arms to LYNN and reluctantly, they begin dancing again.

Next time just ask for another girl, okay? Just tell them to give you any other size 6; they've got lots of them...

SYD
not hearing her
Could you stand a little closer please and, I'm sorry, just turn your face away.

LYNN obeys, moving closer and turning her face away. SYD embraces her more tightly and closes his eyes. They begin to revolve slowly as they dance. There is a silence before SYD whispers to her.

That's right...that's right, dear.

LYNN
quiet emotion
...All those years...just one woman. I mean you hear about stuff like that but...still only her? Still...

SYD
...Still.

LYNN
...Shit...

> *LYNN begins to cry almost silently on SYD's shoulder.*

SYD
> *gently, almost proudly*
Shhhh...it's alright. You don't have to cry for us.

LYNN
> *barely a whisper*
...I'm not...you freak...I'm not.

> *SYD and LYNN continue to dance, holding each other closely as LIGHTS fade.*

> *END OF PLAY*

Bodkin
Robin Russin

Cast
PRODUCER — white, late 20s
WAITER (i.e., actor) — black, large, early 30s

Time
The present

Setting
A restaurant

> *LIGHTS up. PRODUCER sits at a table. He speaks apparently to himself, until it's revealed that he's wearing a Bluetooth.*

PRODUCER
I don't know what to do at this point, I really don't. I mean, this is the third fucking actor to flake on me—one you recommended, I might add. No, he didn't show up. Yeah, yeah, I know, it's a scary role, the greatest role ever written, blah blah blah—but isn't that supposed to be why they all want to do it? I mean, really, "to be or not to be," how fucking hard can that be?
> *listening for a second*

What? No, I haven't read the fucking play. It's written in fucking medieval English or whatever, you think I have the time for that kind of thing?
> *looking around in irritation*

Speaking of which, if this fucking waiter thinks he's going to get a tip, he better get his ass in gear. I been sitting here since the fucking middle ages myself.

> *PRODUCER hangs up as WAITER, a buff black dude in a waiter's apron, enters and walks by.*

Yo—dude! What the hell? What are they doing back there, rubbing sticks together to make the fire?

WAITER
You told me to hold your order, you were waiting for someone—

PRODUCER
Well now I'm waiting for you to bring me my fucking order!

WAITER
Yes sir. "If it be not to come, it will be now; if it be not now, yet it will come: the readiness is all."

PRODUCER
What?

WAITER
Hamlet. I overheard you talking about it. You're a producer?

PRODUCER
Yep. And wait...wait...don't tell me. You aren't just a waiter, you're an actor too. What a shock.

WAITER
I've even played Hamlet before.

PRODUCER
Really? Was it for a Theater for the Blind?

WAITER
Now hold on—it was Shakespeare in the Park—as in New York Central Park—

PRODUCER
Look, dude—I'm sure you're a terrific actor, which is why, after all, you're working at this fine establishment, and I do appreciate the gumption, but let's not go there and embarrass ourselves, alright? In other words, get real, I'm looking for a name.

WAITER swallows his growing anger and puts out his hand.

WAITER
Name's Sam Black.

PRODUCER
ignoring the hand
Black isn't the name I'm looking for, or the look for that matter. No offense, but—
gesturing at WAITER'S overall appearance
—Scandinavian is not what comes to mind. What does come to mind isn't fucking Hamlet, but when you'll bring me my fucking omelet!

WAITER
You know, you're a real asshole.

PRODUCER
I'm a producer, what do you expect? And right now, "to be or not to be" pretty much refers to the state of your tip if I don't get my fucking omelet, you catch my drift?

WAITER leaves. PRODUCER calls after him.

And don't even think about spitting on it or sticking a booger in it or any of that shit—I know what to look for!

PRODUCER gets back on the bluetooth.

Hey. It's me…Who?…No, no way…Look, I keep telling you, I want someone dangerous, someone with an edge…Yes, I know Gibson did it, but that was like a thousand years ago and everyone who even remembers hates him now anyway…But one thing I do NOT want is some prissy Brit like what's-his-name—Brannock? Whatever. I want to play against type—I mean, *Hamlet*—even the title sounds like it's gonna be *Babe, the Return* or something…Look, all I told the studio is that there's a lot of murder and sword-fighting and a guy almost fucks his mother, and they bought the pitch…No, of course they haven't read it. But they want something classy for Oscar season. Now find me someone who can grab this fucking role by the throat and take it someplace no one ever has before!

WAITER returns, overhearing this last bit. He politely sets down the omelet.

About fucking time....

poking at it with his fork

Jesus Christ! Hold on. Look at this. Can you tell me what's wrong with this picture?

WAITER
under his breath

Uh...no spit or boogers?

PRODUCER

It's cold! Ex-squeeze me, but usually when one orders hot food, one expects it to be...hot!

WAITER

I'm sorry, sir. I'll have it reheated.

PRODUCER

The hell you will! You'll have that moron in the kitchen cook a new one, and maybe this time use actual eggs instead of rubber cement!

WAITER reaches for the plate and accidentally knocks a fork into PRODUCER'S lap.

Could you be any less competent?

WAITER suddenly grabs PRODUCER by the throat and lifts him bodily from the chair, taking him to the floor.

WAITER

That's it. I've had just about enough shit from you!

PRODUCER

Are you insane? Do you know who I am!

WAITER

Yeah, and I don't give a shit! You know how long I've been working here, or at a thousand other places just like it, having to put up with crap from jerks like you? I studied at the Royal Shakespeare Company. I have my MFA from Yale. You don't even know the play you're producing!

PRODUCER
Help! Anyone—help!

WAITER
Shut up!

> *WAITER grabs the knife off the table, puts it to PRODUCER'S throat.*

Now the question's for you:
"To be or not to be?
Whether 'tis nobler in the mind to suffer
The slings and arrows of outrageous fortune,
Or—
> *brandishing the knife*
—to take arms against a sea of troubles,
And by opposing end them?"

PRODUCER
Oh, please...please...I don't want to die!

WAITER
"To die: to sleep;
No more; and by a sleep to say we end
The heart-ache and the thousand natural shocks
That flesh is heir to, 'tis a consummation
Devoutly to be wish'd.

> *WAITER drags producer to his feet, backs him up against the wall.*

For who would bear the whips and scorns of time,
The oppressor's wrong, the proud man's contumely,
The pangs of despised love, the law's delay,
The insolence of office and the spurns
That patient merit of the unworthy takes,
When he himself might his quietus make
With a bare bodkin?"

PRODUCER
hysterical
No! Not a bodkin! Not the bodkin!

> *WAITER lets PRODUCER go and tosses the knife aside.*

WAITER
Fuck it.

> *He shakes his head wearily and begins to take off his apron.*

PRODUCER
You're not gonna kill me?

WAITER
No. Just...something I had to get out of my system. A guy can only take so much. I guess I should be used to that by now.

PRODUCER
You assaulted me. You scared the shit out of me.

> *PRODUCER picks up his bluetooth.*

WAITER
So you gonna call the cops? Look, buddy, can't we just let this go? I mean, I think maybe this was a wake-up call for me. I don't belong here. I'll clear out.

PRODUCER
Are you out of your fucking mind? I'm not letting you go anywhere. Not after that.
on phone
Hey. Get over here, right now...Yeah, I did...Yeah, drop everything else. This guy, this fucking waiter no less, fucking knocked me out.

> *PRODUCER hangs up. WAITER sits despondently in a chair.*

WAITER
I didn't hurt you.

PRODUCER
The fuck you didn't, you destroyed me. You got a headshot?

WAITER
What?

PRODUCER
I need to give it to the studio, today.

WAITER
What?

PRODUCER
Dude, are you deaf? I've got the Veep of Production on his way here as we speak. You got an agent?

WAITER
You're...casting me? As Hamlet?

PRODUCER
No, as his mother.

> WAITER *double-takes. Producer slaps his shoulder.*

Dude—of course as Hamlet. That was maybe the most smokin' audition I ever saw. Un-fucking-believable! You actually scared the shit out of me. While doing Shakespeare. You, my friend, are what I've been looking for!

WAITER
But...but...what about...what you said? About me being black?

PRODUCER
Good producer looks beneath the skin. I mean, I've seen them cast Othello as a black guy, that never stopped them.

> WAITER *double-takes at this odd statement, but doesn't have time to dwell on it.*

You're going to be the new face of the Bard's greatest action hero—

> *imagining the billboard*

"*Hamlet*—he's big! He's bad! He's got a bare bodkin, and he's out for revenge!"

> *to WAITER*

So, what are you waiting for? Headshot? Chop chop?

WAITER

Waiting...?

> *He looks down at his apron and starts laughing. So does PRODUCER. WAITER starts to head off stage.*

PRODUCER

Hey, dude—!

> *WAITER turns back. PRODUCER holds up the plate of eggs.*

While you're at it, get me a new omelet. And if you want a tip, try bringing it to me while it's still hot this time.

> *He gets on his bluetooth. WAITER, stunned by it all, takes the plate and exits. PRODUCER speaks to himself.*

Hmmm...What the hell's a bodkin, anyway?

> *LIGHTS out.*

> *END OF PLAY*

Just Because Of The Umbrella
Ivor Martinic

Cast of Characters
TOM — late twenties
ANNA — late twenties

Time
The present, Saturday, early morning.

Setting
A modest living room in the city

> *Modestly furnished living room, in an artistic disarray. There is a sofa in the middle, and some alcohol bottles on the floor. Enter TOM, drunk, and after him, ANNA. They are both uncomfortable.*

ANNA
(*I can see you're mad.*) I hope you're not mad.

TOM
(*And what do you think? It's 2 am.*) No, I'm not mad. I'm just surprised, this late. Have you been waiting long in front of the doors?

ANNA
(*For an hour and a half, stupid me.*) No...ten minutes or so. I was just about to leave. Luckily, I remembered the address. (*Shit!*) I mean, I always remember addresses. Even when I'm drunk.

TOM
(*So, that's how it is.*) And I didn't even remember your name.

ANNA
(*Tom, Tom…*) I didn't remember yours either. I only remember addresses.

TOM
(*Yeah, sure…*) I don't remember anything. I forget names, people, just like that…and honestly, I didn't think you would come back just because of the umbrella.

ANNA
(*Sister's or mother's?*) It's my sister's. I know it's sort of silly but she bought it when she was traveling through Egypt. That was her only trip abroad.

TOM
(*You're a bad liar.*) First trip, you say, and to Egypt of all places?

ANNA
Yes. She won the trip as a prize.

TOM
(*Yeah, right.*) Sure.

ANNA
(*You're not buying it, are you?*) Listen, I should be on my way now. You must have had an exciting evening. Can I have the umbrella?

TOM
Wait, don't go just yet. Take a seat.

> *ANNA hesitates for couple of seconds, but eventually takes a seat.*

ANNA
(*Thanks.*) Okay, I won't stay long…

> *TOM sits next to her. He's looking at her.*

ANNA
(Don't be quiet, you're making me uncomfortable.)

TOM
(Then you say something first.)

ANNA
Were you at Charlie's?

TOM
Yes.

ANNA
How was it tonight?

TOM
(I'd like to fuck you.) Not as good as it was last week when you were there.

ANNA
(I hope I'm not blushing.) Oh, don't remind me. I hadn't gotten drunk like that for ages. I was celebrating my promotion.

TOM
You didn't mention that.

ANNA
(You wouldn't be interested.) When you came, I had already forgotten what I was celebrating.

TOM
And what were you promoted to?

ANNA
(The boss!) Now I'm the head of all the officers in the intergeneration solidarity committee.

TOM
(*I'll laugh later.*) Sounds interesting.

ANNA
(*Of course, you find it extremely boring. FYI, it's a very hard and responsible position.*) It is. We have a lot of work. It's a new committee, and things need to be straightened out. There are so many requests that need to be looked into. It's really unbelievable.

TOM
You look tired.

ANNA
(*Screw you. I put all this make-up on just for you.*) I worked late. And then that party in the neighborhood…I'm sorry, I have no idea why I'm telling you all this. You certainly don't care.

TOM
Come on, relax. There's some whisky there. Pour yourself a glass.

ANNA
No. I'm not drinking tonight. I wouldn't want that thing happening again, like it did last week.

TOM
(*I don't even feel like it anymore.*) It won't. Don't worry.

       Silence.

ANNA
(*Now you're really being rude.*) It would be best if I left.

TOM
You just got here.

ANNA
Just to get the umbrella. I don't want to keep you any longer.

TOM

(*Yeah, sure you don't. Keep lying. Go ahead.*) Oh, come on. Don't you stand there and tell me you're here just because of the umbrella.

ANNA

(*You're being a smartass, aren't you?*) Well, I am.

TOM

What, this late?

ANNA

(*Okay, that's enough.*) Okay, I should really go now. Give me the umbrella.

TOM

(*Now I crossed the line. Wait!*) Please, take a seat. I'm sorry. Don't be mad at me, I'm just silly like that. And don't lie to me either.

ANNA

No...You're drunk. I can't talk to you like that.

TOM

I'm not drunk. Just like you weren't drunk last week.

ANNA

No, I was drunk. I would never, if I hadn't...

TOM

(*Excuses, excuses...*) Yeah...Sure.

ANNA

(*Are you calling me a slut!?*) I don't even know why I came here.

TOM

(*Don't you lie to me. You do know.*) Well, because of the umbrella. You forgot already, did you?

ANNA
Because of the umbrella.

TOM
It's right over there.

> ANNA *walks to her umbrella and notices many different, colorful umbrellas.*

ANNA
I can see you have many ladies' umbrellas here.

TOM
(*Hah, hah…*) Those are my sister's.

ANNA
(*Sure they are.*) Yes. Of course.

TOM
Just like yours is…

ANNA
(*You can tell I'm lying?*) No, mine really is.

TOM
Yes, from Egypt.

ANNA
(*I should have said some other country.*) Yes, can't you see the camels on it?

TOM
Oh look, really, there are camels. And look at that sign down there: *made in USA.*

ANNA
(*Oops!*) That doesn't mean anything. She bought it in Egypt.

TOM

Okay, I won't say a word anymore. *(But I don't understand why is it so hard to tell the truth.)*

ANNA

Okay, I'm off then.

> *ANNA slowly walks to the doors.*

ANNA

You are drunk, and I'm tired...It was nice seeing you. Thanks for the umbrella...*(Stop me, please...)*

TOM

Stop.

ANNA

(Thank you.)

TOM

Hang on for a while. I'm bored.

> *ANNA stops and turns to TOM again.*

ANNA

Hang on to what?

TOM

I mean, stay. Have a drink.

ANNA

No...I mean...okay. *(You're cute...)* You're really unbelievable.

TOM

(Cut the bullshit.) I'm sorry I'm so unbelievable. Take a seat. Whiskey?

ANNA

Okay. I mean…since you're letting me in. Who knows how long the other girls are going to wait to get their umbrellas.

TOM's pouring the drink. He's handing her the glass.

TOM

Don't you worry about the other girls.

They are silent for a while.

ANNA

(*How have you been?*) Have you sold any of the pictures in the meantime?

TOM

(*I haven't been all that well. Same as last week.*) No.

ANNA

If you need some money for the rent, you can tell me…I could…

TOM

You would lend money to a stranger?

ANNA

(*A stranger?*) Well, no…I mean…I would make a contract according to which you would have to pay me back till a certain date. I would protect myself, I wouldn't just do it like that…

TOM

No thanks, it's okay.

They are silent for a while.

ANNA

Are you working on something interesting?

TOM
(I don't know. Maybe.) I'm working on something now. It may turn out okay.

ANNA
There you go. You will sell that picture right away. What's it like?

TOM
(I don't know. It's weird.) It's special.

ANNA
May I see it?

TOM
(No!) No, I'd rather if you didn't.

ANNA
(You're selfish.) Alright. I don't get art anyway, so…

TOM
It's not ready yet.

ANNA
(Don't apologize. I'm not even that interested.) Okay, I get it.

     Silence.

TOM
(I didn't hurt your feelings, did I?) Why are you sad?

ANNA
(Who do you think you are?) Sad? No, I'm not.

TOM
(Oh, come on, stop lying already!) Yes, you are. I can see it in your eyes.

ANNA

(*Leave me alone!*) You're not seeing right. I'm not sad. I have nothing to be sad about.

TOM

But, you are.

ANNA

(*Now we're talking. The masks are dropping off.*) I'm not! Please, don't! Please, don't ask me anything anymore.

> *ANNA gets up. She's nervous.*

TOM

If you want sex, I have no problem with it.

ANNA

(*No, I won't cry*) I am tired.

TOM

(*Don't cry. I'm not good at this.*) I don't understand.

ANNA

I'm tired of guys like you. Listen, we can keep on lying. It's fine.

TOM

I knew you didn't come here just because of the umbrella. Tell me. What's wrong?

ANNA

Don't tell me you didn't feel anything last week.

> *Silence.*

Don't tell me you do that to every girl.

> *Silence.*

Don't tell me it wasn't special, even if it did start off with sex.

TOM
It was good...

ANNA
Don't tell me you didn't like me. Just don't say that.

> *Silence.*

TOM
I liked you.

ANNA
Tell me you have lost my number. Please.

> *Silence for a while.*

TOM
I haven't lost your number. It's right there, on the table, where you left it.

> *ANNA walks to the table and takes a piece of paper.*

ANNA
(*Please!*) Tell me you called me.

TOM
(*I wanted to.*) I didn't.

ANNA
You didn't?

TOM
No.

ANNA
Okay, I just wanted to clear that up. I thought it was my damned machine.... Oh, whatever....

> *ANNA tears the piece of paper with the phone number to shreds.*

ANNA

Now I'm okay. I'm not tired anymore. Isn't that interesting?

TOM

I'm sorry.

ANNA

No, don't apologize. That's stupid. Everything is okay. I just wanted to make sure. That's all. I'm off now. Seriously.

TOM

Stay.

ANNA

No, I have to go...there's no point in staying. *(How can I laugh now?)* Who knows? Maybe there's a man of my dreams standing in the street right now.

TOM

You never know.

ANNA

(That's not funny to you?) Yes, you never know.

> *ANNA gets up and walks to the door. TOM is tense. He's looking at the umbrella.*

TOM

(Forget the umbrella once more....)

ANNA

Goodbye.

> *ANNA stops for a second, and turns around.*

ANNA

I almost forgot the umbrella again.

ANNA takes the umbrella, and TOM'S eyes follow her motion.

ANNA
Goodbye, Tom.

TOM
(Stay. Please, stay.) Goodbye.

> *ANNA heads towards the door.*

TOM
Anna.

ANNA
(So, you did remember my name.)

> *ANNA stops and looks over her shoulder at him. LIGHTS out.*

> *END OF PLAY*

Maude
Mary F. Casey

Cast of Characters
CHANCE — a fifty-year-old lesbian in jeans and a tee shirt
LOIS — a lesbian of forty in a black dress

Time
The present, late afternoon

Setting
A fresh cemetery grave site, Los Angeles, California

> *At rise, CHANCE stands staring at the grave. LOIS enters and stops to watch her for a moment.*

          LOIS
Hi.

> *CHANCE turns, sees LOIS, turns back to grave.*

          CHANCE
Hi.

          LOIS
It was a nice service—

          CHANCE
                overlapping
I didn't hear 'til last night—

          LOIS
                overlapping
Maude would've enjoyed it—

CHANCE
overlapping
I took the first plane out.

LOIS
beat
Hello, Chance.

> LOIS and CHANCE shake hands awkwardly.

CHANCE
Lois.
beat, awkward silence
Hey. Great dress.

LOIS
How could I refuse a dying request?

CHANCE
Maude actually asked you?

LOIS
Not in so many words. I kind of had to figure it out. You know Maude.

CHANCE
Yeah.

LOIS
an awkward beat
I'm glad you came, Chance. I've always wanted to meet you—

CHANCE
overlapping
We've already met.

LOIS
Oh. That was...a mistake.

CHANCE
Well, it was certainly…awkward.

LOIS
I'm sorry.

CHANCE
It's okay. I'm over it.

LOIS
No, I am sorry. You two were still together –

CHANCE
overlapping
Could we not go into this—?

LOIS
overlapping
We shouldn't have—

CHANCE
overlapping
But you did.
> *There is a beat. LOIS is clearly upset.*
Look, Lois, I apologize—

LOIS
No, don't.

CHANCE
This is a horrible time for you and I didn't mean to hurt your feelings.

LOIS
You can't help what you feel.

CHANCE

True. But I could be maybe baseline considerate, given the circumstances, don't you think? A little less of a shitty ex.

> *LOIS nods her head slightly. CHANCE hands her a handkerchief.*

LOIS

You're not…

CHANCE

What?

LOIS

You know.

CHANCE

A shitty ex? Yeah, I am.

LOIS

She loved you for twelve years.

CHANCE

No, we were together for twelve years. She loved me for ten and a half.

LOIS

She never stopped loving you.

CHANCE

In her own way. Don't say it.

LOIS

She loved you, Chance. Believe me, I ought to know.
> *beat*
She left you a letter.

CHANCE

Crap.

> *LOIS hands an envelope to CHANCE.*

LOIS

She made me promise to give it to you.

CHANCE

Bitch.

LOIS

Chance!

CHANCE

Oh come on, Lois. This dying request melodrama shit is vintage Maude.

LOIS

Stop it.

CHANCE

Didn't she just drive you fricking crazy some times? I mean I know you're the grieving widow and all, but you can't be so far gone you don't remember what a complete controlling ass Maude could be.

LOIS

You have no right to talk about her that way. She's dead, Chance. Maude's dead and gone now and you have no right to talk about her that way today, not today.

CHANCE

You just buried the love of my life, Lois, and I have to be on a red eye in a couple of hours because where I work shitty exes aren't covered in the bereavement policy. I have exactly enough time to say goodbye to Maude and whatever the hell I want to you. You may be the widow of record, but my heart is every bit as broken as yours. I just don't get the sympathy cards.

                    LOIS
I'll leave you then.

> *LOIS turns to exit.*

                    CHANCE
Aw, shit, Lois.

> *LOIS begins to walk away.*

I'm sorry. Don't listen to me, okay? I'm being a jerk –

> *LOIS turns.*

                    LOIS
I fought your relationship with Maude when she was alive. I refuse to do it now that she's dead. I don't know what the bond was between the two of you, but believe me I was never able to break it. You were in her thoughts and her heart up until the end.

> *CHANCE opens envelope and reads letter.*

                    CHANCE
Crap.

                    LOIS
Goodbye.

                    CHANCE
> *re: letter*

This is so annoying.

> *LOIS moves away.*

Wait. Come back. Maude's letter—it's a request. And it involves you.

> *LOIS continues to move away. CHANCE has to get in front of her to stop her.*

It's something she wanted me to do with you.

LOIS tries to get around CHANCE who blocks her.

CHANCE
It'll only take a moment.

A beat, then LOIS stops.

LOIS
What is it?

CHANCE
Look, I don't like this any more than you do.

LOIS
Don't like what?

CHANCE
This...this whole thing. Me being here, you being here. Maude not being here. I didn't go to the service for just this reason—I wanted to have a quiet moment with her to say goodbye. But that's shot and now we've got the request to deal with.

LOIS
There are people waiting for me back at the house—

CHANCE
I was hoping to avoid you completely.

LOIS
Thanks.

CHANCE
Wouldn't that have been better?

LOIS
Certainly beats the hell out of this.

CHANCE
I'm supposed to hug you.

LOIS
What?

CHANCE
Maude's request. I'm supposed to hug you and tell you that I hope we can be…friends or something at some point.

LOIS
Friends!

CHANCE
Hey, I told you it was annoying.

LOIS
What was she thinking?

CHANCE
I told you she could be a manipulative ass.

LOIS
God. Just get it over with, okay?

CHANCE
What? The hug?

LOIS
Yeah. Fine. Say whatever you have to.

CHANCE
Let's just do it then and get it over with.

LOIS
Go ahead.

CHANCE
Okay. I'm gonna hug you, Lois, and I'm gonna tell you—

LOIS
Just hurry up.

> *CHANCE hugs Lois awkwardly.*

CHANCE
> *continuing*
Lois, I hope some time we can be…whatever.

> *THEY disentangle quickly.*

LOIS
All right, then. I suppose it could have been worse.

CHANCE
I'm leaving now. You can go back to the house…hey, how's Rocky?

LOIS
He's lost weight. Since Maude got really bad. I can't seem to find anything he wants to eat.

CHANCE
He's been that way ever since he was a kitten, believe me. Try baby food. The kind in the jars. He likes the veal, but that's complicated because you know how Maude felt about factory farming. If it's all he'll eat, though—

LOIS
She'd understand.

CHANCE
Like hell she would. In a pinch he might eat the apricot.

> *CHANCE turns to leave.*

LOIS
Thanks, Chance.

> *CHANCE inadvertently drops letter. LOIS picks it up. She holds it for a moment, looks on other side. CHANCE sees LOIS has letter.*

CHANCE
Oh.

LOIS
There's nothing on this sheet of paper.

CHANCE
It's completely blank.

LOIS
Looks like it.

CHANCE
Well, that's kind of awkward, isn't it?

LOIS
Kind of.

CHANCE
Well, you see—

LOIS
You don't owe me an explanation.

CHANCE
Yeah, I think I do.

LOIS
>   *beat*

Come here.

>   *CHANCE moves toward LOIS who hugs her warmly.*

LOIS
>   *continuing*

I'm so sorry for your loss, Chance.

CHANCE
Thanks.

>   *LOIS hands CHANCE back her handkerchief.*

LOIS
There's a memorial service in June. I wanted everyone from Maude's life to be able to come.

CHANCE
That's a nice idea.

LOIS
So come, okay?

CHANCE
You sure?

LOIS
All the shitty exes will be there.

CHANCE
I can't wait.

LOIS
Seriously, Chance, I know Maude would want you there. So would I.

CHANCE
Okay.

LOIS
Have a safe flight tonight.

CHANCE
I think I may just take an extra minute here to say goodbye, if you don't mind.

LOIS
I don't mind.

> *CHANCE turns back to the graveside. LOIS exits. LIGHTS down.*
>
> *END OF PLAY*

Tied Lines
Amanda LePain

Cast of Characters
BOY
GIRL

Time
The present

Setting
Run down city apartment

> *BOY wakes up, disoriented so it takes a moment before seeing GIRL. GIRL is sitting against the door bruised and bloodied. But the wounds don't appear to be fresh.*

BOY
Who are you?

GIRL
Nobody really.

BOY
> *noticing GIRL's injuries*
What happened to you?

GIRL
Don't you know?

BOY
Should I know?
> *notices blood on shirt*
Jesus Christ is this yours?

GIRL
Some of it could be.

BOY
What the hell does that mean?

GIRL
Some of it could be mine. Some of it might not be.

BOY
Where else could blood have come from?

GIRL
Anyone else who was bleeding.

BOY
Who else was hurt?

GIRL
Maybe nobody.

BOY
Who hurt you?

GIRL
I don't know.

BOY
How can you not know who hurt you?

GIRL
How can you not know if it was you?

BOY
Was it me?

GIRL
I don't know.

BOY
Who are you?

GIRL
I don't remember.

BOY
Stop talking in fucking riddles and answer me.

GIRL
Did you ask me something?

BOY
I've asked you a bunch of somethings.

GIRL
I answered those questions.

BOY
"I don't know" and "I don't remember" aren't answers.

GIRL
They're answers. You may not like them, but they are answers.

BOY
They don't tell me anything, least of all the truth.

GIRL
I don't think either of us knows the truth of this.

BOY
What the fuck does that mean? What happened last night?

GIRL
Nothing happened last night.

BOY
Of course something happened, look at you.

GIRL
Everything ended last night but nothing happened.
pause
I'm going now.

BOY
Go? You can't go.

GIRL
Why not?

BOY
Because you have to tell me what the fuck happened. How I went from drinking at a bar alone to waking up on my floor with a bloody girl sitting against my door.

GIRL
The bar? Is that the last thing you remember?

BOY
Yes. Were you there?

GIRL
Yes.

BOY
How did we get here?

GIRL
A car.

BOY
Before or after you were hurt.

GIRL
After.

BOY
Why did I bring you back here? To help you?

GIRL
Do you tend to help girls that have been hurt?

BOY
No.

GIRL
Then why did you ask that?

BOY
Because I'm trying to figure out what happened.

GIRL
Never ask the obvious. You know the things you would do and the things you wouldn't. I'm going now.

BOY
You're not going.

GIRL
Of course I am. Goodbye.

BOY
No. No. You're not leaving.

GIRL
Why would I stay?

BOY

Because you have to.

> *GIRL starts to leave. BOY grabs GIRL.*
>
> *GIRL fights but does not scream. BOY throws GIRL onto the bed. GIRL stops fighting as BOY ties GIRL to the bed.*

GIRL

You always have such things so handy?

BOY

Tell me about last night.

GIRL

I've told you what I know. Untie me.

BOY

So you can go straight to the cops. I don't think so.

GIRL

If I were going to go to the cops I would have done it after I woke up bloody and beaten. I wouldn't have hung around waiting for you to regain consciousness. So just let me go.

BOY

What did you say?

GIRL

I said let me go . . .

BOY

> *interrupting*

No, before that. If you were going to the cops it would have been when you woke up bloody and beaten. But you said we didn't come back here until after you were hurt so you aren't talking about waking up here. You're talking about when you woke up yesterday. You woke up hurt yesterday which means you were hurt the night before and I remember all of that day so it wasn't me who hurt you.

GIRL
If you say so.

BOY
I do say so. I know what I did that night. And you know what happened to you. People don't just sleep through beatings.

GIRL
You're right. People don't just sleep through beatings.

BOY
What the hell does that mean?

GIRL
How much did you drink last night?

BOY
A couple beers.

GIRL
Always been such a lightweight? A couple beers and you black out.

BOY
I never black out.

GIRL
Gee, that's fascinating.

BOY
You know who drugged us.

GIRL
Did I say we were drugged?

BOY
You insinuated it.

GIRL
And there's the heart of our dilemma. All I can do is insinuate. I don't really know any more than you. I have my suspicions—my theories, but I don't really know anything. You want me to lay out all of last night for you. Explain how A led to B led to C led to girl tied on bed but I can't.

BOY
Then give me your theories.

GIRL
No.

BOY
Little girl, I am losing patience with your games and the mockeries you call answers.

GIRL
Gee whatever will you do when your patience runs out? After this, what can your next moment possibly be?

BOY
I don't understand.

GIRL
Bullshit. End this before it comes.

BOY
What does that mean? What do you think is next?

GIRL
You disappear.

BOY
Threats now?

GIRL
A little late for me to start that don't you think? I'm just trying to give you some perspective. Flash ahead ten hours from now. I'm still tied up. Still haven't told you what I don't know or what I don't want to say. After all that time what do you think will be left for you to do?

BOY
You think I'll kill you.

GIRL
Or seriously consider it.

BOY
And then I'll disappear. In what sense?

GIRL
In the sense that I am the last line you haven't crossed.

BOY
How do know the number of lines I've crossed? Or that I haven't crossed that one?

GIRL
They wouldn't have put me here otherwise.

BOY
They, they, THEY!! Fucking tell me who they are.

GIRL
I DON'T KNOW WHO!

BOY
You said they!

GIRL
Of course I said they. What else am I going to say? Someone had to have
done all of this. If it really wasn't you and let's face it, you're not actually
that certain about it, but if it wasn't you then someone had to beat me up.
Someone had to spike your drink. Someone had to put us here together.
Someone. Them. They. Those are the only words I can use. I can say
nothing more descriptive than that.   '

BOY
Sure you can, give it a shot.

GIRL
Odd choice of words.

BOY
I could say the same about yours. Most people in your position wouldn't
be the first to mention killing. Doesn't seem wise.

GIRL
It's not my job to be wise.

BOY
What is your job?

GIRL
I'm the bloody girl by the door.

BOY
I know that.

GIRL
No you keep overlooking that.

BOY
Meaning.

GIRL

Meaning you keep looking past me. You keep looking out there, to whoever put me here and why they did it. But none of that matters. I'm the bloody girl by the door.

BOY

Why you? Who got you involved?

GIRL

Doesn't matter. It doesn't matter if someone is trying to prove someone else wrong about you or if someone is trying to confirm their long held beliefs about you or if someone is merely having fun. It doesn't matter if I was involved from the start or dragged into it. All that matters is we're here. I'm the line. I'm the bloody girl by the door.

BOY

Stop saying that.

GIRL

What else can I say? You have tied me to a bed. Your anger is rising, becoming dangerously close to lashing out. Not sure with what, more words, fists, knives, guns. But lashing out, that's inevitable. You refuse to let me go or believe anything I'm saying. But despite that I will again boil the story down for you. I'm the fucking bloody girl by the door. Finish it.

BOY

How can I finish what I didn't start?

GIRL

Of course you started it. You started it the first time you told a lie to get more ice cream. You started it the first time you stole a pack of gum from a store or cheated on a test. You started it at eighteen when you seduced your fourteen-year-old neighbor. And there was no turning back after you threatened your father with a shotgun. But the cherry on top was breaking parole to stalk your ex.

BOY
How do you know all that?

GIRL
Maybe I don't. Maybe I guessed it all. Maybe you're as transparent to me
as the air. Maybe I've been in situations like this before. Maybe even on
your side. Maybe I've crossed that line. It's not about that. It's not about
me. I'm only the question.

BOY
Do I kill?

GIRL
Yes.

BOY
You're the bloody girl by the door.

GIRL
I'm the bloody girl by the door. But am I the corpse at your feet?

BOY
Seems like there should be more options.

GIRL
There aren't.

BOY
That's the thing you're willing to be so definite about.

GIRL
What else could you possibly see me as? Redemption?

BOY
Let's assume my sins are too great for that.

GIRL
Am I a second chance?

BOY
I'd only make the same mistakes.

GIRL
Then what else can I be?

BOY
Not sure but there has to be more. Maybe they know.

GIRL
Who?

BOY
Whoever's coming next.

GIRL
Nobody else is coming.

BOY
You sure?

GIRL
Never.

BOY
Then we'll wait.

GIRL
And if someone else does come?

BOY
I don't know.

BOY goes to the door and sits against it just as GIRL was in the beginning.

END OF PLAY

The Trunk of Turin: One Small Act of Faith

Andrew Davis and David Dolle

Cast
TERRY
PAUL

Time
The present

Setting
Near the trunk of a car

> *The stage is dark. Stage right is the trunk of a car. Two men enter stage left and talk as they walk to the trunk.*

TERRY
Miracles, Paul, miracles.

PAUL
Miracles? I don't have time. I don't need miracles. I need a ride to the clinic.

TERRY
We all want to believe in miracles, right? Don't we? I mean not normal everyday miracles, waking up, sunrises, smiles on babies...I'm talking about pyrotechnical extravaganzas...blazes of light...something outta nothing miracles...a miracle where you don't have to go to the clinic—

PAUL
> *cuts TERRY off*

Whatever you're selling, I can't afford. Okay, Terry? Whatever scheme you're hatching I want no part. I want to be at the clinic on time so leave the sparkling verbal bullshit in the car...listen, all I need is a ride to 9th and Division so I can see a doc; can you do that for me? Can ya?

> *PAUL starts walking away.*

TERRY
Yeah, I'll do that.

> *PAUL stops and turns.*

PAUL
Okay, then let's go...

TERRY
But first...

> *TERRY presses the button on his key chain and the trunk lid
> pops open. When it does there is a soft golden light from inside.
> PAUL snorts, walks over, looks in.*

TERRY
You recognize him?

PAUL
He looks familiar...

TERRY
Jesus Christ.

PAUL
Swear all you like...I just can't place him.

TERRY
You idiot, he's Jesus Christ.
> *points into trunk*
There!

PAUL
It is, huh?...You put the savior in the trunk of your car?

TERRY
No, I found him there.

PAUL
You found Christ in your trunk?

TERRY
So it seems.

PAUL
How did Jesus get in your trunk?

TERRY
I don't know.

PAUL
Is he…dead?

TERRY
I don't think so.

PAUL
What are you going to do?

> *TERRY shuts the trunk.*

Huh?

TERRY
I think, right now, the two of us knowing he's in my trunk is enough.

PAUL
But it seems kinda…

TERRY
Yeah, I know, closing Jesus in the trunk…I'm pretty sure I'm going to hell for that.

> *PAUL and TERRY stand and look at the closed trunk for a minute.*

PAUL
Maybe, it's just a dead hippie.

TERRY
> *cocks his head*
He's not dead, he's sleeping. And he's not just some hippie. He's Jesus…King of the Jews.

PAUL
And Jesus is sleeping…the Son of God needs to sleep?

TERRY
Sure, when he's tired, and when he's in human form, you know, with all the afflictions of being mortal. You know: pain, hunger, weariness, thirst…maybe he could use a beer.

PAUL
Okay Terry, the savior does not need a six pack.

TERRY
I said maybe, maybe he gets thirsty. He did take human form so he could experience humanity, to face and defeat temptation…
> *TERRY's voice trails off.*

PAUL
Where did you get all that?

TERRY
I went to Sunday school.

PAUL
So did I, but I don't remember anything about Jesus hopping into someone's trunk for a nap; not even the Popemobile.

TERRY

Jesus is poppin' up everywhere. Tree bark, cookies, wallpaper, ham and eggs. They're selling him on Ebay. Hell, tell me where he isn't. He's God, he can do anything he wants.

PAUL

I don't want to be having this conversation?

> *TERRY clicks the button again and the trunk opens. The light glows.*

TERRY

That's why we're having this conversation.

PAUL

> *creeps closer to the trunk and looks in*

He hasn't moved an inch. Are you sure he's just asleep? Did you check?

TERRY

Well, not really.

PAUL

So we really don't know...

TERRY

He doesn't look dead.

PAUL

And you know what a dead God should look like?

TERRY

Well, not really.

PAUL

And you drove all the way here from your place?

> *TERRY nods.*

And he didn't wake up? Didn't move? Didn't yell "LET GOD OUT OF THE TRUNK!"?

TERRY
Well, no.

PAUL
So, he might be dead.

TERRY
Well, I guess so.

PAUL
Close the trunk.

> *TERRY steps up and closes the trunk. He steps back to stand by PAUL. Both men just stare at the trunk lid.*

PAUL
Maybe it's just some guy that looks like Jesus.

TERRY
Maybe...

PAUL
But you don't think so, do you?

TERRY
No, I think he's the real deal.

PAUL
I'm not even convinced there is such a thing as the real deal.

> *PAUL and TERRY just stare at the trunk for a minute.*

When did you find him in there?

TERRY

This morning. I opened the trunk to throw in a bag and he's there. He wasn't in there last night. But today, I open the trunk and, big head rush with the light.

PAUL
shaking his head
I'm not quite ready to buy the fact that Jesus is in your trunk.

TERRY
But he is.

PAUL
steps forward and shuts the trunk
I still think it could be some guy that looks like Jesus...

TERRY
And how did he get in my trunk?

PAUL
I don't know. Where was your car?

TERRY
In my mom's garage, ever since I got back from the bar last night.

PAUL
You went drinking, drove home, put the car away, and then "pop" Jesus is in the back.

TERRY
Yep.

PAUL
When was the last time you were in the trunk?

TERRY

Yesterday afternoon, I bought a twelve pack and didn't want it sitting in the back seat while I was in the bar.

PAUL

So, it had to be while the car was in the garage or parked at the bar…

TERRY

Well not at the bar…I remember I put the beer in after the bar and there was nothin' but greasy stale air.

PAUL

So, somewhere between the bar and your mom's garage he snuck in.

TERRY

I think Jesus can just appear where he wants to.

PAUL

I'm still not sure this is Jesus…and I'm not sure he's still alive….. What if he is dead?

TERRY

Jesus can't be dead.

PAUL

Follow me for just a minute…what if it isn't Jesus, and what if he is dead…you got a dead guy in your trunk. Maybe we should call the police.

TERRY

Uh…I don't know if that would work. I'm still on probation for that thing with the baseball bat…

PAUL

And the three bags of home grown?

TERRY

Yeah, that little thing. So if it isn't Him, and if he is dead, I'd like to have some better explanation than, "I don't know."

PAUL

Good idea. But right now, I got nothing for you, buddy.

TERRY

And to think you're the smartest guy I know.

PAUL

You're screwed.

TERRY

No, I'm fine.

PAUL

How do you figure?

TERRY

Because it really is Jesus.

> *PAUL shakes his head again. TERRY pops the trunk. The light shines.*

See…

PAUL

I saw.

TERRY

No, really look. Check him out; he's wearing a robe.

> *PAUL steps up to the trunk and looks in. He stares down into the glow. After a few seconds he turns and looks at TERRY, then back into the trunk. PAUL closes the trunk.*

PAUL
Okay, maybe, but how can you be so sure?

TERRY
I don't know, but I know. It was this morning, that head rush, I just knew after that. I have...faith.

PAUL
smiling
Oh man, you're gonna be a Bible thumper.

TERRY
I guess, except I don't own a Bible.

PAUL
Pop the trunk again.

> *TERRY pops the trunk and there is no light. Paul looks in.*

PAUL
Jesus Christ...

TERRY
I knew you'd see it.

PAUL
No, Terry, he's gone.

TERRY
What?
rushing to the trunk
Nooo...
looks in
Where did he go?

PAUL

I have no idea. I wasn't even sure he was there until a couple of seconds ago.

> *TERRY closes the trunk, opens it again. No light. He does this three or four times until PAUL reaches out and touches his arm. The trunk lid is left open and he steps back.*

TERRY

I thought he was for real.

PAUL

I know, I saw him....can't blame it on drinking...I haven't drank in days...you know, because of the clinic.

TERRY

Why did he go?

PAUL

You gotta have faith now. That's why he left. If he was here it would be easy to believe, but with him gone, we have to have faith.

TERRY

We?

PAUL

Yeah, we.

TERRY

When he was here, you didn't.
> *perplexed*
Now he's gone, and you do?

PAUL
> *laughing*
Yes, I guess so.

> *PAUL steps up and looks in the trunk again.*

Hey, look at this.

TERRY
moving to the trunk, looking in
Wow, that's kind of strange.

PAUL
Was it there before?

TERRY
I don't think so. I just got this a month ago; and the used car guy over on Jackson had it cleaned up pretty good. I don't remember it.

PAUL
It's right where he was laying. It's like an outline.

TERRY
Like the shroud of Turin—I got the trunk of Turin now?

PAUL
At least the Shroud in the Trunk of Toyota.

TERRY
Nope, not buying that.

PAUL
Why not, couple of minutes ago you believed that Jesus himself was napping in the trunk. Now you don't believe that he can leave a mark.

TERRY
Nope, cause you know what that makes me? Do you?

PAUL
No, what does that make you?

TERRY

Crazy, like that old lady that had Jesus on her toast. People will figure it's some kind of scam. I'm not doing a scam on this one. That's all I need, a whole new pile of crap in my life. When it was Jesus in the trunk he was going to explain it. Now I have to...nope, not me. Not on this one. Don't have enough crazy.

PAUL

But the mark is there.

TERRY

Looks like a small, dark, something. Could be oil, could be anything. Nope, this was all some kind of bad drug.

PAUL

But I saw him.

TERRY

A delusion. You shared my hallucination.

PAUL

Did not.

TERRY

Hang on.

> *TERRY reaches into the back seat pulls out a 40 of beer. Shakes it, sprays the beer into the trunk. Shuts the trunk*

No more Shroud of Toyota. Okay, enough of that. What are you going to do?

PAUL

I don't know. This is going to take some thinking. A little bit ago I had nothin', now I think I might want religion.... What about you?

TERRY

I am going to pretend none of this happened. It'll be easier.

PAUL
Really?

TERRY
Really. We'll get some pancakes; you can say grace.

END OF PLAY

Outside of Competition: Bonus Tracks

In the true tradition of Fn Productions, each event dictates that somewhere we throw out rules and do what we Fn want. Also, E-MergingWriters.com strives to include "bonus selections" in all of our printed work. What better bonus than two more tried and true (and critically loved) 10-minute plays worth staging?

Our first bonus feature is Murray Scott Changar's play *White Picket Fence*. It would be easy to dismiss this work as a gimmick or write it off as a scene written for shock value, but that would be sophomoric and wrong. The play is a testament to our culture and the dialogue, though seemingly stilted, sings out as if two adults are trying their best to dance gracefully across crackling ice before reality sinks them. Also, to dismiss this scene is to deny that it happens every day.

Last summer, we discovered our second bonus selection, the irresistible work of Charles Borkhuis, floating around the edgier theatres of New York. Charles' dual hats of poet and playwright allow him access to the existential and to the voice as song in ways other playwrights only dream.

We hope you enjoy them both.

White Picket Fence
Murray Scott Changar

White Picket Fence was produced by Atlantis Playmakers for their Short Attention Span Play Festival in Boston, 2006.

Cast of Characters
MAN — late 30s, 40s, business attire, slightly overweight, mundane appearance with a successful salesman's manner whose smile never leaves his face
WOMAN — late 30s or much older, either the BOY's mother or grandmother, poorly-dressed but as well as she can manage
BOY — 14 years old, a bit vacant, a bit slow, does what he's told, but does not respond to the events of the play

Time
Summer, now

Setting
A motel room somewhere

> *WOMAN is seated. MAN is seated near a table. BOY is standing near the door, a small suitcase at his feet.*

WOMAN
What a very nice room. Very nice. You in these parts often, Mister?

MAN
No. Not really.

WOMAN
Well, if you're ever back, I sure do hope...you will—

MAN

Oh, of course. Business takes me all over. I'm the Region 4 man. Up, down. Back and forth. Company Rep for 16 states.

WOMAN

You hear that, child? Why, Mister here is a successful business man. I…I'm so sorry, how'd you go and say your name again? Mister, I'm just plain horrible about names!

MAN
slowly
Bronstien. Bob Bronstien. Spelled with the "i-e" but say it with the "e-e."

WOMAN

Oh. Bronsteeeeeeen. That's a eastern name, isn't it? Joshua! Sit down right now, please, and stop fidgeting. And wipe your face.
hands BOY a handkerchief
Thank you! Now sit down on the bed.

MAN

That's right, son. Go on. Be comfortable. Hot as holy heck out there.

WOMAN
Mister, it sure is.

BOY sits.

Joshua's a good boy. Aren't you, Sweetie?! Most times he's no trouble at all. What did you say…was your line of work?

MAN

Tubular steel. All shapes, all sizes, all purposes. Folks don't realize, you know, how necessary…. Let's just say our pipes are used in everything from sewers to spaceships!

WOMAN
Oh, my.

MAN
Much of the business now is plastics and custom concrete. Company's called Tubular Steel, but if it's any kinda tube you need, we'll make it.

WOMAN
Sounds like a good living to me. A very good living.

MAN
Yes. Yes it is. I'm with them 20 years come next spring.
There is a long, uncomfortable pause.

WOMAN
Well, my acquaintance…, Mr. Schaefer…? He said that—

MAN
Mr.—? Oh! Sure. Sure.

WOMAN
Dick Schaefer. He said that you would want to…get right to it. That you were…a very…*honest* and…that you were someone to trust.

MAN
Absolutely.

WOMAN
You know, I work for the county here. Bunch of years, and…well, that's not my only job. I just want to make sure that…

MAN
pause
What did Dick Schaefer tell you…exactly?

WOMAN
pause
That I could depend on you. What we agreed to, I mean. What him and me talked about—you would see it through.

MAN
Guaranteed.

WOMAN
I been tellin' people that Joshua might be goin' away. A special school. Everyone here knows what me and the boy can and cannot afford. Lord knows there ain't nothing 'round here right for him. So I says, it's a federal grant, and we got that grant through the county. 'Cause I worked for the county so long.

MAN
That's just fine. All they need to know.

WOMAN
But Mister, what I'm trying to...Mr. Brown-steeen. What Dick Schaefer didn't tell me about was ...*is*...where Joshua and you...will be living at? For my peace of mind and such?

MAN
No.
　　　　　Long pause as WOMAN tries to speak. MAN shakes his head.
That's just not a good idea.

WOMAN
Oh! Well. I'm afraid I don't know what to say. I just...I....

MAN
Now, look. I cannot tell you that. I never will tell you that. As for Josh, I *will* tell you, the best facilities in the whole country are not far from me— from where we'll be. I've spoken to them. Started the process; made the arrangements. What's more....

WOMAN
That's nice, Mister! That's real good!

MAN
What's more…is…I can afford it.

WOMAN
Yes.

MAN
Easy. So, let's get down to it. Shall we?

WOMAN
Yes.

> *Long pause as MAN's fingers tap the table.*

MAN
So…what else Dick Schaefer tell you?

WOMAN
That you were a *generous* man. And an honest….

MAN
Yeah. Okay. Okay.

> *MAN crosses the room, picks up a briefcase, returns to the table,*
> *pulls out an envelope.*

WOMAN
We're very grateful, Mister. I just know that things are gonna…work out
fine.

MAN
> *opens envelope*

What I got here is a bank check. You can see that…oh, sorry, let me turn it
around. You can see that this check's drawn from a national bank—got no
name on the top—my name's not there, just the bank's name. And no city
is on there neither. That's how I do my business. You won't have no
problem with this here check, alright?

WOMAN
> *reacts to the amount*

Thank you, Mister.

MAN

And they're gonna keep comin'. Ya hear me? Not this big, of course. This here's a one-time-only check. Every month you're gonna get one of these. In your mailbox. And that little thing in the corner—the postmark?—that's gonna change—'cause I'll be on the road. You'll get your check every month. 'Til the boy's eighteen. Then it stops. No more money. You understand?

WOMAN

Yes, Mister.

MAN

I'll bring him 'round every Christmas and you're gonna have a week with him. That's once a year.

WOMAN

Alright. Alright! We're gonna have Christmas, Joshua!

MAN
> *slowly*

Now, I have to make one thing absolutely clear. You cannot...you will not speak about this to anyone. No one's gonna hear about this arrangement. Not your friends, not your brother, your sister, the neighbors, folks you work with. Not nobody.

WOMAN

Mister, I don't have—

MAN

Do you know what a breach is? A breach of contract? Do you know what that is?

WOMAN
Well, I…think I do.

MAN
Breach of contract means you have broken the arrangement; our arrangement. Means you have injured me by doing that breach. It means the money will stop.

WOMAN
Yes, sir.

MAN
And you'll never see this boy again. I promise you that. Now I don't know much about Dick Schaefer. But I know enough. You get lonely for the boy and go talkin' to Dick, or talkin' to anybody at all about our arrangement—then that's a breach—and he'll let me know. You make inquiries about me or my business—I'll know. But if you take my check, this here check—that means you agree with what I'm saying. Do you agree with what I'm saying?

WOMAN
Well, yes Mister. I guess I do.
                    pause
Uh…what happens if…if I….

MAN
No, ma'am. Just ain't gonna happen.

WOMAN
Oh.

MAN
Nothin's gonna happen. Go on. Take the check. It's yours.

> *WOMAN rises slowly and takes the check. She looks at it carefully, folds it, tucks it into her handbag, then sits down near the BOY.*

WOMAN
I reckon the child's got what he needs. In his suitcase. His clothes and whatnot. Medicine. And Mister...he likes those Oreo cookies.

MAN
Alright.

WOMAN
He'll start fussin' if he don't get 'em.

MAN
Alright.

WOMAN
Don't know how to thank you. Guess I'm doing the right thing.

MAN
Of course you are. Now you take some time—all the time you want—say your good-byes. Take that check right to the bank.

WOMAN
Yes, sir. I will.

> Long pause as WOMAN looks at BOY, fondles his hair, then abruptly goes to the door. She turns, about to speak to BOY, but reconsiders.

MAN
Did you see out the window there, ma'am?
> she turns to MAN

Just wanted to let you know that that car out there? That blue car? That's not mine. I'm not parked anywhere near here. If you happen to notice on your way.

WOMAN
Oh! I would never....

MAN

That's fine. Now you go on to the bank.

WOMAN

Yes. Yes, I will. Thank you, Mister...I...forgot how you say your—

MAN

That's just fine.

> *WOMAN smiles, lets herself out.*

> *MAN, still seated, turns to face BOY.*

Wasn't my name, anyhow.

> *There is no movement as LIGHTS fade out.*

> *END OF PLAY*

Present Tense
Charles Borkhuis

"In *Present Tense,* the confining space accentuates a claustrophobic, existential atmosphere, which I tried to use in both frightening and humorous ways. The thin white poles that boxed off the performance space resembled some of painter Francis Bacon's tortured interiors, and I was determined to use this to my advantage by having the characters confront the audience directly through the "bars" of their captivity. The time and location of the play were set as the performance time on location at the Brick Theater. Themes of presence and absence and living double lives played nicely into these confined quarters by allowing the two characters to find themselves "slipping" in and out of parallel lives through "wormholes" in the space-time of the play. MAN ONE believes he has dozed off at home with a book on his lap and the play is a curiously lucid dream. MAN TWO is convinced that their performances in front of a live audience are desperately real. Panic starts to set in as the play's complications and reversals become increasingly fascinating and frightening. After seeing Gabriel Shanks' marvelously stark, droll production, I decided to use *Present Tense* as the opener in a four scene, full-length play, called *Stage Fright.* "
 – *Charles Borkhuis*

Present Tense was produced at the Ontological Society's Tiny Theater Festival at the Brick Theater in Brooklyn, May 2008, which requires a 6'x6'x6' space restriction; hence, the name. The play was directed by Gabriel Shanks, featured Frank Blocker and Ben Trawick-Smith, with stage management by Jeni Shanks and design by Allen Cutler.

Cast of Characters
MAN ONE — 40s
MAN TWO — 20s

Time
Performance time of play

Setting
A wormhole in space-time

> LIGHT on MAN ONE asleep in a white chair under a mosquito net, upstage. A red clock sits on a white pedestal, downstage. LIGHTS up on MAN TWO, entering upstage. He notices ONE and stops. He turns slowly to audience and smiles self-consciously. His smile wanes; he becomes anxious. He breaks his stare and goes to the red clock, picks it up, and checks the time. He winds the clock, sets the alarm, and places it back on the pedestal. He returns to ONE and stares at him.

TWO
> *whispers*

It's time.

> Pause, then TWO nudges ONE slightly. No response. TWO gives the audience a sheepish grin and turns back to ONE.

It's time!

> Pause, then suddenly fearful, TWO nudges ONE harder. ONE moves.

ONE

What?

TWO

Time! The clock's been set.

ONE
> *disoriented*

What...clock?

TWO

Our clock. Time is ticking, even as we speak. Perhaps you're not sufficiently...
> *staring at audience*

Here. With us, right now.

> *officious*

I do not know where you go when you're not here. All I know is: If you are not here, we cannot...begin.

ONE

I *am* here. You have my undivided—

TWO

We cannot begin unless you are...indisputably—

> *A beat, then TWO removes the mosquito net from ONE in one quick motion. ONE is reading. Beat. He turns a page of the book.*

ONE

> *looking up*

Ah, I'm afraid you caught me.

> *smiles, closing book*

Reading again. It's the only way I can fall sleep. The letters get heavy. They slide down the page like bullets...and I nod off into small visitations. Sometimes I glimpse people I've never seen before. Just a moment ago, I spied a giant, smiling couple drinking cokes on the TV sky between buildings. The woman spoke to me personally. "You'd never do anything to make us ashamed of you, would you?" I turned around and an old woman stuck a red clock to my forehead. I stared at my ticking reflection in a mirror and the hotel room turned into a tiny stage. Someone was asking me questions. I believe...it was you.

> *turning to audience*

There was an audience present. They were laughing.

TWO

Wishful thinking.

ONE

Maybe.

> *beat*

I must admit...

> *turning away*

I have a hard time looking at them. The naked fact that their stares are nailing us to the floorboards doesn't fill me with dread. Far from it. I want to run out and kiss them just for being here—NOT!

TWO
What's your problem?

ONE
I know what they're thinking.

TWO
What are they thinking?

> *ONE and TWO stare at audience.*

ONE
When will this be over?
> *beat*
I've already said too much.

TWO
You've hardly said anything.

> *ONE stands, putting the book on the chair. He turns to TWO.*

ONE
Maybe I've...left my sleeping body back there, and what you see before you is my second body on an extended...leash.

TWO
Pull yourself together, will you? The audience is watching us for signs of inauthentic behavior.

ONE
What does that mean?

TWO
Bad acting.

> *ONE sits on stage, looking at audience.*

ONE
Maybe it's true, maybe we are, at this very moment, addressing an audience of decent, socially and ecologically-minded humanitarians. Of a sort.

> beat

They wouldn't hurt a fly. But are they *real?* you might ask. Not me. I've been here before, trapped in a dream I couldn't talk my way out of. Awake inside it, perfectly lucid, but unable to leave.

> *ONE points toward the chair. LIGHTS dim, special on chair, bright.*

In point of fact, I am sitting in my favorite chair in the living room of a secluded central Pennsylvania farmhouse. I've just dozed off with a book on my lap. I'm dreaming this right now. My wife is sitting in her favorite chair opposite me, reading *The Phenomenology of Science* by Hans Jonas. There are logs burning in the fireplace and our Weimariner is sleeping on the Navajo rug next to us. I am a playwright between plays. Our two sons are upstairs doing whatever it is teenagers do when they think their parents aren't watching.

> *LIGHTS brighten.*

TWO
I've got a suggestion: suppose you restrict yourself to the situation at hand. That being: We are actors, facing an audience that is waiting for a play to begin. Remember, the clock is ticking. When the alarm rings—

ONE
What alarm? What play?

TWO
As if you didn't know. So…if you are truly present, we can begin.

ONE
Maybe we've already begun without knowing it.

TWO
> *sigh*
I doubt that.

ONE
Maybe everything starts and ends in the middle. Maybe nothing ever quite finishes, or ever really begins.

> *ONE picks up the red clock and checks the time. He puts it down and turns to the audience.*

ONE
I must say…as far as dreams go, this is all very convincing. In fact, it's one of the most lucid dreams I've ever had. Everything appears…seductively real. But of course, the bubble may burst when I wake up.

TWO
How can you be so sure you haven't already woken up? We are, in point of fact, at the [name of theater] in [city]. Outside there are real people with real problems dragging up and down [street name]. Take it up a magnification, and there's an entire city beyond that, and a country beyond that, and the earth beyond that, and the entire universe beyond that, and perhaps an infinity of universes beyond that.

ONE
Sounds real…dreamy. So what's your stake in all this?

TWO
I'm an actor. So are you. We have a calling.

ONE
Who's calling us?

TWO
We're professionals, for Christ's sake. We can do this. Finish what we started.

ONE
I'm not so sure there's an end to any of it. It's all wormholes in the fabric, one moment to the next.

TWO
People are living real lives out there!

ONE
Don't bet on it. What's your real life like?

TWO
Acting is my life. It's what I do.

ONE
So, where do you live?

TWO
                unsteady
What?

ONE
What street do you live on?
                beat
Do you live alone?
                beat
Who's your closest friend? Do you have roaches?

TWO
                weakly, backing up
Strange, I...

ONE
Where's your closest police station? Do you love anyone? Does anyone love you?

TWO
            becoming dizzy
I don't, ah—

ONE
Remember? That's all right. You don't have a real life outside this theater, do you?

            TWO starts to collapse. ONE catches him under the arm.

ONE
I know what it's like: One world curled up inside the other like so many extra dimensions.

            ONE leads TWO to the chair and removes the book.

TWO
I'm feeling…a little light-headed.

            TWO sits down.

ONE
Relax. What do you want, you're still acting, aren't you?

TWO
Am I?

ONE
Of course. Tonight we improvise! Ha, ha!

TWO
But what about the audience?

ONE
They're still here.

TWO
Yes, but—

ONE
Listen, in this dream, everything is true to life. Look at them.

Someone in the audience coughs.

They cough, they breathe, they break wind. Every so often, there's a little titter, a laugh, a frown. What more do you want?

TWO
I want them to be real! To have lives outside this –

ONE
Why can't they just be what they are? A memory, a sliver of a thought curling inside our heads. Even...even at the moment of perception, the present is always something of a memory. How else would we recognize it?

ONE hands TWO the book.

TWO
nervous
But what happens when the alarm goes off? Will you wake up? Will I disappear?
regarding the audience
What about them? Will they remember us?

ONE
Difficult to say.

TWO
rising weakly
What about you? Will you remember me? Our time together, here upon the old boards?

TWO reaches out for ONE.

ONE
Of course, I'll remember you. Sit down.

ONE helps TWO back into the chair.

I'll have a good laugh over this with my shrink. He'll ask "Who is this new friend of yours? How do you feel about being with him on stage in front of an audience? Why do you need this confirmation that you actually exist?" Of course, he will use this dream as a lever to explore my feelings about not having been born sufficiently. Or perhaps, explore my suspicion that I'm already dead.

TWO
Of course, It's all about you. It's your dream. But what are...what are the assurances that you'll remember any of this?

ONE
Assurances are difficult to come by.

TWO
So, it could turn out—
                defeated
—that I never existed.

ONE
I am not a stranger to such thoughts.

> *ONE turns away. TWO rises out of his chair and tries to strangle ONE, but ONE overcomes him and pushes him to the floor.*

TWO
        panting
You're trying to...kill me!

ONE
Don't you think I could say the same thing about you?

> *Beat. ONE takes a small bottle of pills and a flask out of his pocket and gives them to TWO.*

Take this. We all need a little mother's helper sometimes. Go on. Don't be a child about it.

> *TWO takes the pill and gulps from the flask. He returns them to ONE.*

TWO
I'm sorry I tried to strangle you. It's…not like me.

ONE
It was an exciting moment for everyone, but now it's already history. Here…

> *ONE picks up the book from the floor and hands it to TWO.*

ONE
Try reading this. Put you right out. Does wonders for me.

TWO
You understand, don't you? How the panic can sneak up on you and suddenly without warning, grab you by the throat?

ONE
Yes. I've been in your shoes. Or shoes like yours.

> *TWO opens the book and starts reading.*

TWO
> *reading*

"ONE is asleep under a mosquito net. TWO enters and notices ONE. TWO smiles at audience self-consciously."
> *yawning*

This sounds familiar.

ONE
Go on.

TWO
> *reading*

"TWO's smile wanes. He becomes—
> *becoming sleepy*

—anxious, uneasy..."

> *ONE walks downstage, stops at the red clock and picks it up.*
> *TWO drops off to sleep but suddenly wakes up, reading:*

"He...he goes to the clock and checks the time."

> *TWO falls asleep. ONE returns the red clock to the pedestal.*
> *ONE drapes the mosquito net over TWO.*

ONE

It's time.

> *ONE walks downstage and smiles at the audience.*

We know each other, don't we? You're my witnesses. You still feel incredibly real to me. Does that make you feel any better? Perhaps not.
> *serious*

Shall I take your silence as a sign? Of what?
> *beat*

One hears voices. They never stop...Have I created you in my own image? Why should I care if anyone is watching? Why did he care?
> *turning to TWO*

Where is he now? So far away.
> *beat*

Sleep slips us the false feeling that we somehow know death. We don't.
> *to audience*

I dreamt you up, didn't I? For my own purposes. Maybe that's why I don't trust you. Who knows what you're thinking? When I look at you, I can't help feeling the weight of the world descending.
> *closing his eyes*

I can't quite—
> *violent gesture, opening his eyes*

—rid myself of you! There, you see? Why can't I dream of something else? Why do you keep coming back like a personal haunting? Suppose there is no other world to return to? What happens to my wife and children, waiting for me to wake up? I was happy there! Completely....

solemn

But suppose I don't wake up…back there, and instead end up here, in this world with you. And my other reality, my real life is over. How could it be over?

LIGHTS have faded on TWO.

Please forgive me. I know…you can't respond. It's not your role. One talks and the other remains silent. For eternity. But which one is talking and which one is silent?

beat

I'm afraid I've become desperate.

to himself

Oh, have a little dignity, won't you? Play out your part. That's all anyone can ask. Play out your part! Pull yourself together, man.

to audience

Excuse me, I must look like I'm having a nervous breakdown. I'm not, really. It's just my face.

smiling

There, that's better.

more controlled

When the alarm rings, I will not go out…screaming. I will not….

smiles fades

Still, one never knows when the time comes whether there will be a scream or not. But what I do know, what I'd stake my life on, is that at some time, at some place, this has happened. And that we have formed a bond.

looking across the audience

Surely, I can't be mistaken about this.

> *TWO whimpers and moans in his sleep. ONE turns back to TWO and takes a step towards him. SOUND: alarm rings loudly. ONE freezes in his tracks. LIGHT up on TWO as he "wakes" in the chair. He puts his hands over his ears and gives a silent scream that freezes on his face. The alarm continues as ONE pivots his head back slowly and stares steadfastly at the audience. LIGHTS fade to black.*
>
> *END OF PLAY*

Biographies [1]

Playwrights

Joan Anderson and **Dorothy Sanders** (*I Witness*) have been writing plays together for more than fifteen years. Their work has been produced on various stages and chosen as a finalist or winner in several national competitions. Joan is a communications/marketing specialist, actress, children's book author and an award-winning journalist and video producer. Dorothy is a well-known actress on area stages, the dramaturg at Circle Theatre in Fort Worth and a founding director of Artisan Center Theater in Hurst, Texas.
Contact: andblock@aol.com (Joan Anderson) and allenandot@yahoo.com (Dorothy Sanders)

Alex Broun (*Beer and Newspaper*) has enjoyed considerable success in theatre, television and film as a writer, actor and director. He has had many plays performed in the United States, South Africa, Singapore, the United Kingdom, Taiwan, Malaysia, the Philippines, and Australia. A specialist in ten-minute plays, in recent years he has had more than 40 short plays produced in more than 150 productions across the globe. He is currently Director of Short & Sweet Sydney and Brisbane (Australia) 2009. He has also recently launched a new website offering downloads of many of his plays, free of charge.
Contact: www.alexbroun.com

Charles Borkhuis (*Present Tense*) is a playwright, poet, screenwriter, and essayist. His plays have been performed in New York City, Los Angeles, San Francisco, Hartford, and Paris. *Mouth of Shadows*, a collection of his full-length plays, was published by Spuyten-Duyvil. His CD *Black Light* contains two radio plays produced for National Public Radio and is available on www.pennsound.com. He is the recipient of a Drama-Logue Award, a critic's choice in the Los Angeles Times, and the former editor of Theater:Ex, an experimental theater publication. Books of poems include the following: *Afterimage, Savoir-Fear, Alpha Ruins, Dinner with Franz, Proximity (Stolen Arrows)* and *Hypnogogic Sonnets*. *Alpha Ruins* was selected by Fanny Howe as a finalist for the William Carlos Williams 2001 Book Award. His latest book of poems is *Disappearing Acts*, forthcoming 2009.

Contact: 104 E. 4th St. – D1, NY, NY 10003, cborkhuis@aol.com, 212-473-1744

Hugh Cardiff (*The Librarian*) works in information technology and has had short plays produced in Ireland, the United Kingdom, Malaysia, Singapore, and Australia. He was also short-listed in the 2006 RTÉ (national Irish Radio) annual P. J. O'Connor Radio Drama Award for new writing.
Contact: hcardiff@gmail.com

Mary Casey's (*Maude*) full-length play, *Unspeakable Acts*, was the 2008 winner of the Jane Chambers Playwriting Award. Her full-length play, *Women and Horses and A Shot Straight From the Bottle*, a 2000 finalist for the Jane Chambers Award, received its world premiere at Echo Theatre in Dallas, Texas, 2006, and was nominated for three Leon Rabin Awards through the Dallas Theatre League. Her play, *Buck and Bean*, was a finalist for the 2007 Heideman Award at Actors Theatre of Louisville. She is a proud member of the Dramatists Guild of America.
Contact: mcplywrt@aol.com

Wm. P. Coyle (*Faith*) is a poet, playwright and fiction writer. He has published work in numerous journals. His poetry can be found in *Broken Bridge Review*. In January 2008 his short play *Living Room*, inspired by the mixed-media installment of the same name by Richard Jackson, was performed as part of the "Size Matters XXL: Image and Script" Festival at the Hudson Valley Center for Contemporary Art in Peekskill, New York. His full-length play, *Eight Lines*, was a semi-finalist in both the 3rd Annual GreenHouse Playwriting Competition, sponsored by HotCity Theatre in St. Louis and City Attic Theatre's CAT Tales Competition. He is also a theater critic for Offoffonline.com, a website that primarily reviews Off-Off Broadway and Indie Theater in New York City.
Contact: williampcoyle@hotmail.com

Murray Scott Changar (*White Picket Fence*) spent his life in pursuit of performing, seeing and encouraging great theatre. Directing credits include the off-Broadway productions of *Nelson and Simone: Out of Senses* and *Full Circle*. He has written one full-length play, *The Gates of Helen* (Atlanta, Georgia, Whole World Theatre, 2004). His one-page play *The Old Actor and the Whore* was produced by Lamia Ink and his 10-minute plays

include *The Noble Sons of Popeye*, performed by Circus Theatricals of Los Angeles, and *White Picket Fence* which was performed by Boston's Atlantis Playmakers for Short Attention Span Play Festival and by New York's 4th Meal Productions. All plays written by him have found their way to the stage. Murray Scott died March 21, 2008, leaving behind his cherished partner Frank and his beloved kids Teheché, a German shepherd-mix adopted from the ASPCA and Gracie, a Himalayan cat. And he probably would have dedicated his play's appearance in this book to Doofus, Lucy, Camelot and Freedom since he's playing with them right now.
Contact: e-mergingwriters.com or email nyplaywright@gmail.com

S. L. Daniels (*Night Vision*) was born in London, raised in Toronto and Los Angeles, and currently lives and works in Chicago. Her play *Rain, River, Ice, Steam* was produced in Chicago at the Tony Award-winning Victory Gardens Theatre in Los Angeles, at Moving Arts Theatre, and in New York at the West End Theatre. Other work has been produced in Chicago by American Theatre Company, Mary-Arrchie Theatre, Rivendell Theatre Ensemble, and Live Bait Theatre, and in New York at the West End Theatre, Samuel Beckett Theatre, and Harold Clurman Theatre. Recent readings/workshops have taken place at A Red Orchid Theatre (Chicago), American Theatre Company (Chicago), and Victory Center Theatre (Los Angeles). Credits also include winner of the Illinois Artists Award for Playwriting, winner in the Samuel French One-Act Competition, winner in the 2008 Theatre Oxford Short Play Contest, and finalist for Actor's Theatre of Louisville's Heideman Award, the O'Neill Playwriting Conference, and the Cunningham Prize. Television and film work include the Canadian animated sit-com, *Committed*, co-writer for the HBO IND/FOX TV show *ROC*, executive script consultant on *Workout*, a pilot for NBC, and writer of the short film *Mr. Peach's Dinner Party*.
Contact: sldaniels7@hotmail.com

Andrew Davis and David Dolle (*The Trunk of Turin: One Small Act of Faith*) Dave Dolle was born near the Mississippi River and now lives in La Crosse, Wisconsin. A man of varied experience, he tries to enjoy a single, full and dramatic life. He earns his living in the health care field, but it's only a job. Andrew Davis was born in the bottom land of Illinois but now lives just a little way from the river in Houston, Minnesota. He, his wife, and their son live in the country and enjoy every minute of it. He, too, has a job that pays bills but lets him work at his writing. They met at a writer's group that meets in the basement of the public library twice a month. **Contact:** Andrew Davis, 17119 County Road 26, Houston, MN 55943, 507-896-4854, rvpub@acegroup.cc **Contact:** David Dolle, 814 King Street, Apt. 2, La Crosse, WI 54601, 608-796-1582, davedolle@yahoo.com

William Gebby (*The Right Not to Take Me Seriously*) started writing scripts twelve years ago. His one-act play, *Incense for Shiva*, was a winner of Indiana University–Purdue University Fort Wayne's Indiana Voices Competition in 1997. His full-length play, *A Lynching in Southern Indiana*, played to critical and popular acclaim at Theatre on the Square, Indianapolis, 1998. His ten-minute play, *1918*, was produced by Theatre Studio Inc., New York City, 1999. Close to a half-dozen of his plays have received public readings by The Indiana Theatre Association and The Algonquin Project. From 2002-03, he served as publicity director, stage manager, assistant director, and producer at Center Stage Productions, Indianapolis. In 2003, he founded Inklings Theatre which produced three of his plays: *The Confessional*, *The Geranium*, and *A Prayer for the Dead* (2004). In 2007, *War To End All Wars* was featured as part of The Indianapolis Theatre Fringe Festival. He received a Basile Theatre Fellowship the same year. In 2008, he was a finalist in The Kairos Prize Screenwriting Competition. A lifelong Hoosier, he lives in Indianapolis with his wife and two children.

Beth Kander (*Psychic*) teaches playwriting and theater classes, has had several short stories and essays published, and has worked as a journalist and a screenwriter. Her plays and monologues have been workshopped and performed throughout North America, including at the London Fringe Festival, Flint City Theater, and Mississippi State University. Her first full-length drama, *Unshelved*, won second prize at the 2008 Eudora Welty New Play Series, New Stage Theatre of Jackson. She is a board member of Fondren Theatre Workshop and Offkilter Comedy, both of Jackson, Mississippi. Her undergraduate degree is from Brandeis University and her Master's is from the University of Michigan. While waiting for her big break, Beth still has a day job. Recent honors include winning the 2009 Mississippi Theatre Association Playwriting Award and being named the 2009 Best Jackson Writer by the Jackson Free Press. **Contact:** beth_kander@yahoo.com

Steven Korbar (*All the Way, A Slight Limp-The Later Life and Adventures of Tiny Tim*) works as an actor and playwright in the Los Angeles area. His full-length and one-act plays have been produced at Theatre of NOTE, Sacred Fools, Little Fish, Write/Act Repertory—all Los Angeles—and Cleveland Public Theatre and North Park in San Diego. His ten-minute, *Our Little Angel*, was published as part of *Stage This, TOO!* and his short comedy, *I Understand Your Frustration*, won Best Production at "8 Minute Madness" in New York City in 2008. Steven's new full-length comedy, *Third Bull Run*, will receive its first reading in early 2009.
Contact: stevekorbar1@juno.com

Robert Paul Laudenslager (*All the Pretty Little Horses*) holds a Bachelor of Arts in Theatre Arts from Virginia Tech where he began his career as a playwright, actor and director. He primarily writes small cast plays for college theatre ensembles and college audiences, including his plays *Soh*cah*toa* and *Spoke*, which have been produced at the Virginia Tech Blackbox Theatre. Readings and workshops of his plays have included *All the Pretty Little Horses, Blacksburg I'm Dead, Happy Endings*, and *I Am Bryan Breau*.
Contact: rlaudenslager@gmail.com

Amanda LePain (*Tied Lines*) is a playwright and performer originally from a small town outside of Worcester, Massachusetts. She attended Ithaca College where she received a Bachelor of Arts in Drama. After graduation she relocated to Minneapolis, Minnesota, where she currently works in Audience Services at The Children's Theatre Company.
Contact: slater410@yahoo.com

Ivor Martinic (*Just Because of the Umbrella*) was born in Split, Croatia, 1984. He has published poetry and prose in periodicals and worked as a television script-writer and CvD editor, has written scripts for short features and experimental movies, and worked as a journalist for Hollywood magazine (Croatia). As a dramaturg, he has worked on plays for theatres including Theatre &TD, Small Scena Theatre, Zagreb Youth Theatre and Children Theatre Dubrava. In 2003, he won the Matrix Croatic Award for best prose piece. For his dramatic text *Simply: (unhappy)* he was given the Marin Drzic award by the Croatian Ministry of Culture, making him the youngest winner in the award's history, and his play *The title of the*

drama about Ante is written here won the Fabriqué en Croatie award. The play was performed on Croatian radio and in concert (directed by Rene Medvesek) at the International Drama Colony organized by the international ITI centre, at the 15. Eco Heritage Task Force (International Colony) where it was directed by Slaven Spisic, and at Blue Elephant Theatre, directed by Rebecca Tortora of London. It was also produced by City Theatre Split, directed by: Ivica Simic. Radio plays include *Without a title, Return* and *Past,* broadcast on Croatian, German and Hungarian radio. He is a graduate student of dramaturgy at the Academy of Dramatic Art in Zagreb. Other plays: *A Nun, a Boy and other passersby* (2006), *A play about Mirjana and those around her* (2007).
Contact: ivor.martinic@gmail.com

Marie Mastrangelo (*A Peace of Candy*) grew up in Los Angeles. After graduating from Scripps College with a Bachelor of Arts in music and drama, she moved to New York City to pursue singing and acting. She appeared in several Off-Broadway productions and toured with the singing group Rudy's Jukebox. Fifteen years later, she found herself back in Los Angeles writing screenplays. Her play *Wasted Wishes* was the inaugural production for the Chance Theater in Orange County. She was also a finalist in The British Short Screenplay Contest.
Contact: mariegavein@dslextreme.com

Michele Merens (*Geraldine*) is a writer and playwright with the following credits: production of her full-length drama, *The Lion's Den*, in Milwaukee, Wisconsin funded by a grant from the Puffin Foundation (2008); publication of a play and short stories in *Lilith Magazine* (2008) and *Crawdad* (2007, 2006); 10-minute play readings at Great Plains Theatre Conference (2006) and Chicago Dramatists (2004); semifinalist in Princess Grace Playwriting Competition (2008), LakeShore Players (2007), Mildred and Alfred Panowski Playwriting Competition (2003); "Golden Dozen" recipient for column writing, International Society of Weekly News Editors (ISWNE, 2001). She is a Barnard College Senior Scholar and member of Dramatists Guild of America.
Contact: comeonin@wi.rr.com

Robin Russin (*Bodkin*) is a professor screenwriting at University of California, Riverside. He was educated at Harvard, Oxford, RISD, and University of California-Los Angeles, where he taught for six years before

joining University of California-Riverside. Robin has written and directed for film, TV and the stage, and written articles and reviews for various national publications. He is the co-author with Bill Downs of the books *Screenplay: Writing the Picture* and *Naked Playwriting.*
Contact: Associate Professor, Screenwriting, Department of Theatre, University of California at Riverside, Riverside, CA 92521, robin.russin@ucr.edu

Paul Shoulberg's (*Gone*) play, *Reel*, premiered as part of Indiana University's main stage season in December 2006, was performed at the Pabst Theatre in Milwaukee, Wisconsin, as part of the American College Theatre Festival, and was the winner of the Kennedy Center's 2007 Mark Twain Playwriting Award for Comedy. His play, *Dying on the Vine*, was a semifinalist for the 2008 O'Neill Theatre Conference as well as the 2008 Julie Harris Playwright Competition. His play, *Tweaked*, received 2nd Place in The University of Tulsa's New Works For Young Women Competition and was the runner-up in Stony Brook University's 2006 John Gassner New Play Competition. His play, *Slip, Stumble, Fall*, was selected for the The Willows Theatre's NextFest and was a finalist in HotCity Theatre's New Play Competition. He received his Bachelor of Arts in Theatre and Film from Kansas University and his Master's of Fine Art in Playwriting from Indiana University
Contact: 3951 Gouverneur Ave. Apt. 2K, Bronx, NY, 10463, (785) 766-7488, thedogcantalk@gmail.com

Alan Steinberg (*Cosmic Judo*) works at the State University of New York (SUNY) Potsdam and over the years has published fiction including *Cry of the Leopard* by St. Martin's Press and *Divided* by Aegina Press, poetry including *Fathering* by Sarasota Poetry Press and *Ebstein on Reflection* by Idaho State Press, and the drama *The Road to Corinth by* Players Press.
Contact: 13 River Drive, Potsdam, NY 13676, 315-267-2008, steinbal@potsdam.edu

Lisa Stephenson's (*Cheryl, JD*) accomplishments include the following: Production Assistant/Broadway/TV: *The Philadelphia Story*, *Macbeth*, Woody Allen's *The Floating Light Bulb*; *Aren't We All?* (with Rex Harrison and Claudette Colbert); *Wild Honey* (with Sir Ian McKellen); *Blithe Spirit* (with Geraldine Page and Blythe Danner); and *Sweet Bird of Youth* (with Lauren Bacall); *Night of 100 Stars II, Triple Play* (with Liza Minnelli).

Playwright/Freelance Writer: *Very Soon and in Pleasant Company* (Theatre 22, NYC); Theatermania.com; *The Manhattan Times*. Education: Bachelor of Arts in Theatre/English; post-graduate tutorials at Christ Church, University of Oxford, United Kingdom. Memberships include Dramatists Guild of America and the MacDowell Society.
Contact: #611, 1815 Wm. Howard Taft Road, Cincinnati, OH 45206, ZT@Fuse.net

Asher Wyndham (*Barsha Badal*) is a dual citizen of Canada and the United States. In 2005, he graduated from the University of Sioux Falls, South Dakota, with a Bachelor of Arts in English. In 2007, he attended the Edward Albee New Playwrights Workshop at the University of Houston where he studied under Lanford Wilson. He has studied playwriting at Columbia University and continues his graduate study of the craft at Arizona State University, Tempe. His works include the following: *Daniel(le)* (Orlando GLBT Festival; Bryant Lake Bowl Theatre, Minneapolis); *Mere Midwest Trucking* (New Workshop Theatre, Brooklyn); *The Next Marlon Brando* (Cabaret Theatre at the Temple of Music and Art, Tucson); *Fugly* (Cabaret Theatre, Tucson); *Veteran Silas* (Wordsmyth Theatre Company, Houston; University of Houston); *Sisterhood School* (New Workshop Theatre, Brooklyn); and *Love Sofa* and *Father Aschenbach* (Live Theatre Workshop, Tucson). He is a member of Old Pueblo Playwrights and Dramatists Guild of America.
Contact: sinoraboy@yahoo.com

Editors

Frank Blocker's plays include *Eula Mae's Beauty, Bait & Tackle* (off-Broadway, 2001), *Southern Gothic Novel* (Drama Desk Solo Performance Award nomination, Broadway World's Audience Favorite Award nomination, Columbus Theatre Festival, Left Out Festival, Stage Left Studio, NY Fringe Festival, Baltimore's Sky Room), *Patient Number* (Inner Voices Social Issues One-Act Play Winner/University of Illinois), *Suite Atlanta* (78th Street Studio Theatre), *Kiss and Fade* (Short Attention Span Play Festival, Boston), *The Wisconsinners* (Dubuque Fine Arts Center), *Air Marshals, Chameleüns* (co-authored with Rochelle Burdine) and book for the musical *Alice* w/ composer William Wade (The York Theatre Development Series, Emerging Artists Theatre's Notes From a Page). As

an actor, Frank has appeared with Peculiar Works Project in their Obie-award winning production of *West Village Fragments/East Village Fragments* and as "the last Don" in *The Don Quixote Project*. New York credits include Roderick Usher in Steven Berkoff's *Fall of the House of Usher*, Mortimer in Brecht's *Edward II*, and most recently in *The Beggar's Opera* as Mr. Peachum. Frank manages the website PlaywritingOpportunities.com (visited by thousands of visitors each month), is a member of The Dramatists Guild of America and a member of Actors' Equity Association. He is an honors graduate of Cameron University and studied theatre and writing at Southeastern Oklahoma State University. He lives in Manhattan with his dog and cat.
Contact: nyplaywright@gmail.com or www.frankblocker.com

Dana Todd is considered one of the luminaries of internet marketing and travels the globe to speak at conferences and seminars about the topic. She launched an early boutique interactive agency, SiteLab, and an internet advertising network, Newsforce. She also helped found the Search Engine Marketing Professional Organization (SEMPO) and served as a Board member and Chairperson, among other roles. In her early life, she was a journalist and editor for several regional newspapers including *Savannah News-Press* and *Mesa Tribune*. She lives in San Diego, California, with an incredibly overweight cat and searches for the next big thing in media.
Contact: dtodd@newsforce.com

Sydney Stone made her feature film debut in the indie flick *In The Flesh* by Ben Taylor. Originally from Atlanta, Georgia, Sydney studied acting at The University of Alabama-Birmingham, then moved back to Atlanta continue studies at The Alliance Theatre and The Warehouse Actor's Theatre. While in Atlanta, Sydney performed in *Crimes of the Heart*, *The Unexpected Guess*, *Greetings* and Alan Ball's *Five Women Wearing the Same Dress*. She also starred in several indie films including *Tech Support*, *Manchild* and *Creep*. Sydney made her NYC stage debut in Eve Ensler's critically acclaimed play *The Vagina Monologues* in 2004. An animal lover and activist, Sydney is a proud supporter of many animal charities, including the ASPCA and the Humane Society of the United States.

---

[1] *Biographical data was provided by the playwrights.*
* *Member of Actors' Equity Association, Union of Professional Actors and Stage Managers*
‡ *Member of Dramatists Guild of America*

Cast and Crew from 2007 *Stage THIS!* Performance and Reading

One dozen of the Stage THIS! published playwrights were granted a three-week Equity showcase production at the 78th Street Studio Theatre in Manhattan, December 6-22, 2007. The remaining winning playwrights received a staged reading on the afternoon of December 22, prior to the final performances. A play's selection for either production or for reading was based on actor and technical availability, meaning we wish to make no quality distinction between those plays produced, and those that were read. Following is a list of each play's participants:

Production

Whatever Happened to...The Three Sisters (Audience Favorite) by Bill Cosgriff of New York, New York, directed by Murray Scott Changar and starring Stacie Theon, Sydney Stone* and Heather Koren*

The New Wife (Audience Favorite Runner-Up) by Wendy Foerster of Arroyo Grande, California, directed by Iftiaz Haroon and starring Emilie Byron*, Brian Distance and Heather Koren*

Night Nurse (Audience Favorite Runner-Up) by Cara Vander Weil of New York, New York, directed by Sydney Stone and starring Stacie Theon and Frank Blocker*

Blue-Collared Dreams by Jon Tyler Owens of Atlanta, Georgia, directed by Jon Michael Murphy and starring Eric C. Bailey* and Moti Margolin

Goodbye, New York by Greg Tito of Brooklyn, New York, directed by Mark Finley and starring Moti Margolin, Sydney Stone* and Frank Blocker*

Johnny Ramirez Really Wants to Kiss Me by David-Matthew Barnes, McDonough, Georgia, directed by Jon Michael Murphy and starring Bobby Abid and Chris Von Hoffman

The Last Box by J. Michael Harper of Fayetteville, Arkansas, directed by Cara Vander Weil and starring Emilie Byron*, Moti Margolin and Chima Chikazunga

Moonshine on the Rocks by Jeffrey James Keyes of Milwaukee, Wisconsin, directed by Frank Blocker* and starring Charnele Crick, Bobby Abid and Heather Koren*

Our Little Angel by Stephen Korbar of Torrance, California, directed by Cara Vander Weil and starring Eric C. Bailey* and Sydney Stone*

Piney Ridge by La'Chris Jordan of Seattle, Washington, directed by Murray Scott Changar and starring Charnele Crick, Chima Chikazunga, Emilie Byron* and Brian Distance

Saturday Night Newtown, Sunday Morning Enmore by Alex Broun of Australia, directed by Iftiaz Haroon and starring Stacie Theon and Frank Blocker*

Terror, Astonishment, Love by Evelyn Jean Pine of San Francisco, California, directed by Halina Ujda and starring Charnele Crick, Frank Blocker*, Brian Distance, Chima Chikazunga, Chris Von Hoffman and Heather Koren*

The Stage Manager was Yan Wu and the Technical Director was Kenneth Allen.

Staged Reading

The Dark by Janice Kennedy of Los Angeles, California, performed by Stacie Theon, Bobby Abid, Charnele Crick and Chima Chikazunga

Feeding Mr. Why by Craig DeLancey of Fairport, New York, performed by Moti Margolin, Eric C. Bailey* and Frank Blocker*

The Night the Widget Broke: An Almost True Story by Mark Castle of Birmingham, Alabama, performed by Gina Bonati*

Orange Sunset by Vicki Riba Koestler of Alexandria, Virginia, performed by Emilie Byron*, Brian Distance and Heather Koren*

* *Member of Actors' Equity Association, Union of Professional Actors & Stage Managers*

About E-Merging Writers, Fn Productions and PlaywritingOpportunities.com

E-Merging Writers is a collective of theatre artists seeking to promote playwrights and new works. Artists include playwrights, writers, composers, dramaturgs, directors, producers and actors. Founded in 1994 as a website for blogging—before "blogging" was a word—the site began offering detailed listings of playwriting opportunities and soon became the most comprehensive listing on the web for playwriting options in development, residencies, workshops and contests. The group has continued to evolve, publish, produce, and the site PlaywritingOpportunities.com welcomes 5,000 writers a month to access free information regarding where to send their work.

Based in New York City, Fn Productions is a relatively young theatrical production company, developing from the desire to provide actors with new works and established plays that people want to see. The company produced an Equity showcase of the 2007 Stage THIS! winners, several private readings of new scripts, and an Equity showcase of *Suite Atlanta*, in its first year. Fn Productions is a theatre company commercially producing new works that are, dare it be said, entertaining.

Online: http://www.EmergingWriters.com
                 http://www.FnProductions.org
                 http://www.PlaywritingOpportunities.com

By US mail: E-MergingWriters.com/PlaywritingOpportunities.com
                 411 E. 90th, 1E, NY, NY 10128
                 Fn Productions,
                 87 Crans Mill Road, Pine Bush, NY 12566.